T-SHIRT MAGAZINE PRESENTS

LAUNCH A KICK-ASS T-SHIRT BRAND

AN ESSENTIAL GUIDE
TO BUILDING A T-SHIRT EMPIRE

PRODUCED AND PUBLISHED BY

T-SHIRT
MAGAZINE

For information, address
T-Shirt Magazine, 50 Harrison Street #212J, Hoboken, NJ 07030

www.T-ShirtMagazine.com

Designed by AJ Camara

ISBN: 978-0-615-52384-2

Printed in the United States of America.

A SPECIAL THANKS

To T-Shirt Magazine's hardcore fans and all of our contributors who helped make this book possible.

TABLE OF CONTENTS

INTRODUCTION

So you want to start a t-shirt business. Congratulations on choosing a challenging and rewarding business venture in which to unleash your creativity. In this world, there are few things more satisfying than seeing your t-shirts worn by people all over the world. People who are willing to give up their hard-earned cash for something *you* made. Becoming the next big thing is every aspiring brand owner's dream.

Unfortunately, just dreaming about starting a successful t-shirt brand is not enough. You have to take action to make your fantasies come true. Whether you've been an artist and designer for years or have no artistic talent whatsoever, starting a t-shirt business is an ongoing process that requires a lot of hard work and devotion.

Years In The Making

Our journey to launching a kick-ass t-shirt brand has been several years in the making and will probably be somewhat similar to yours. It should give you a scope on the creation of a successful brand from its earliest stages.

The Beginning

Several years ago, before launching *T-Shirt Magazine*, we created a comic book we planned on selling in major comic shops. Along with the comic, we created t-shirts based on the characters from the comic and sold them online. At the time, we created and sold our products through an all-in-one fulfilment company called *Cafe Press,* which required little to no money to launch and maintain. This was the first time we created an entire collection of t-shirts, and we actually sold a few too.

Okay, honestly, when I say we sold a few, I really mean *few*. Granted, t-shirts weren't our main focus at the time, but since we were still developing the comic, we weren't satisfied with the results of our business—especially since we only profited about $3 for each t-shirt we sold through Cafe Press. We also had to put the comic book on hold because we had to raise more funds to publish it. We planned on doing this through selling more t-shirts.

The Launch of T-Shirt Magazine

Soon after our first t-shirt endeavor, we developed the idea of T-Shirt Magazine. Through this publication, we started sharing our experiences selling through Cafe Press, in addition to anything else we knew so far, while expressing our enjoyment of t-shirt design and culture via articles and blog posts. We simultaneously launched a limited-edition t-shirt brand available exclusively on the website.

The plan was to release a new t-shirt each week, but unfortunately, we didn't sell a single one. We created and attempted to sell these t-shirts through a Cafe Press competitor site called *Spreadshirt*. With no upfront production costs and relatively low maintenance, we figured we'd go with the cheapest route.

Since the beginning of T-Shirt Magazine, we started interviewing up-and-coming t-shirt brands on a weekly basis to give other emergent designers inspiration. At the same time, these interviews inspired and educated us as well. We further educated ourselves on the development of these brands and the aspects that played into their success. We became t-shirt brand experts of a sort, knowledgeable on nearly every aspect of creating an awesome t-shirt brand. Or so we thought.

Our First Official T-Shirt Brand

Our next venture was creating a whole new t-shirt brand unrelated to T-Shirt Magazine or anything else we were running at the time. At this point, the comic book we were working on was long forgotten. However, we did get one copy created, which is sort of like an artifact now. With our first official t-shirt brand we decided we wouldn't use Cafe Press, Spreadshirt or any other fulfilment company this time.

After studying many of the brands we had interviewed through T-Shirt Magazine, we realized they were doing things we were incapable of doing by selling through a fulfilment company. Custom labeling, jumbo screen-printed designs, hang tagging—you name it. Almost anything that makes a t-shirt cool we realized we just couldn't do with a fulfilment company. So, we had no choice but to do it on our own this time if we planned on making it big. And doing it on our own meant start-up costs, product development, and fulfilling orders ourselves.

We were barely out of high school at the time and had no jobs, so we were pretty much too broke to fund everything we planned for. We created seven t-shirt designs to be printed on

American Apparel t-shirts and planned on custom-packaging them with a few other extra goodies in each order (a strategy we learned from some of the brands we'd interviewed). We convinced our dad that we had an excellent business idea and needed help funding it, and so the first season of our first official brand was released.

The first season was the last season. We were perplexed. We had everything planned out, we had set goals and planned daily tasks to get where we wanted to get, but all we could sell was 20-something shirts to our friends and a handful of fans on **Myspace**. After a few months of slow sales, we began developing the second collection, and during the development the idea of a new brand came to mind: **Cashletes**.

Our Second Official T-Shirt Brand

My gut feeling was to stop the first brand completely and start developing Cashletes. Hundreds of ideas came to me in an instant, and I knew we had to go with this new concept. This time, I did even more research on not only what goes into developing a t-shirt line, but what goes into developing a solid brand. We tried to make sure not to repeat any of our mistakes from the past, and we built this new brand with care and precision, using some tools and resources we had discovered over time.

Signs of Success

Fast forward to the present, and we definitely consider the Cashletes brand a success so far, even though we haven't reached all of the pinnacles we plan to reach. We know our t-shirt brand is kick-ass because we now make thousands of dollars every month selling through more than one channel, and we have a fan base all over the world, with customers in countries we've never even heard of.

We have celebrity stylists contacting us, frequently requesting products for their clients to wear, and retail shops begging to get a hold of our stuff to sell in their stores. We've kept the brand alive through several collection releases and have even expanded to getting clothing custom-made overseas. We're also glad to say we even have our own office. Something we could only dream of a few years ago.

An Essential Guide

Our story might sound like what you'd hope to achieve soon, and chances are you will if you take smart steps. We created this guide because we get questions from our readers all the time about specific concerns that we realized hadn't been sufficiently answered anywhere else—concerns that we, too, had throughout our journey. We hope to address these questions and more throughout this guide.

To make this guide even more helpful, we enlisted the help of a few other founders of kick-ass brands who really know their stuff, some of whom have achieved way more success than we have so far and were nice enough to share their wisdom and their own stories. Pay close attention to these exclusive brand owner contributions highlighted throughout the book, as they are probably the most important passages you'll read. After reading this book in its entirety, we truly believe you'll be on your way to launching a kick-ass t-shirt brand of your own.

1

REALITY CHECK

Many people have this crazy idea that starting a t-shirt business is easy. The truth is, starting a t-shirt business is far from easy. If you're looking for the quickest route to get rich while putting in little effort, look elsewhere. In fact, both successful and aspiring t-shirt entrepreneurs alike will tell you that launching a successful t-shirt business can be extremely hard. Sorry to break it to you, but they're right.

It's Tough Out There

With all the new t-shirt brands popping up every day, it's no surprise that many people believe it doesn't take much work to set up shop and start making money. Starting a successful t-shirt business is just like starting any other business. It takes, among several other things, willingness, dedication, skill and, whether you like it or not, money. There are going to be times you'll feel like throwing in the towel, too.

Even after we had been at it for a while, there were still months we had to rummage for loose change for lunch money, and we thought maybe it was time to give it up, maybe it just wasn't worth it. But you know what? We kept on going, and that's what set us apart from most aspiring business owners who fail in less than a year.

Think You Got What It Takes?

Before you dive deep into the business, you need to seriously think about it and decide if this is the business for you. Are you truly passionate about creating a t-shirt brand? Are you ready, willing and able to sacrifice other important things in your life for your business? Are you ambitious enough to set goals and climb the ladder to success? Or are you just doing this for the money, or because you thought it would be cool to have a clothing line?

Don't give up on your dreams just yet. Only you can truly decide if you have what it takes to make it in the business. If you believe so, it's likely that you'll do whatever you have to do to make things happen, and reading this book is a big step. But in addition to being mentally prepared for this venture, you have to be financially prepared. Starting a t-shirt business is neither easy nor cheap. If you thought you were going to magically start a business and actually make money without spending any money, you've been misled. Know your finances, and be ready to spend time and money.

A Lot To Learn

While starting a brand is its own reward, sometimes you yearn for a little more. If your goal is to become a successful t-shirt entrepreneur, or even a t-shirt millionaire, this book will give you the information you need to set yourself apart from the slew of other aspiring t-shirt entrepreneurs out there with the same goal. You will learn how to research the market, get your t-shirts printed and ready for sale, and acquire press coverage for your brand online and offline.

From developing your ideas on paper to producing and selling them to earn money, there is a lot to learn. This book contains a wealth of knowledge to set you on the right path to accomplishing these difficult tasks while having fun at the same time.

So you want to start a kick-ass t-shirt brand? Are you ready for the exhilarating journey of running your own business? Well then, read on!

2

STARTING POINT

The prelude to this kick-ass guide is an informative article on *T-ShirtMagazine.com* titled "10 Tips For Launching Your T-Shirt Business," which has become the most-visited article on the site. Since then, our inbox has exploded with emails from aspiring brand owners asking us for more advice. This article serves as a good starting point for anybody launching a t-shirt brand. If you have already read it, it's always good to refresh your memory.

To kick off the hundreds of pages of priceless tips and advice that follow, here's the article that started it all.

10 TIPS FOR LAUNCHING YOUR T-SHIRT BUSINESS

It seems nowadays that everybody is selling t-shirts, and if you haven't started already, you might be next. Before you jump into the t-shirt business, you might want to take a few pointers, and we've got you covered. Here's a guide on how to start your own t-shirt business, divided into the 10 most important aspects.

1. Do Your Research.

Make sure you're knowledgeable about the clothing industry before you dive in. Get an understanding of how the business works. Read about how other brands became successful and model a similar strategy.

2. Plan Everything.

Before you get started, have a clear idea of what you plan on doing. Try to decide things like what kind of t-shirts you will be selling, who your target market is, whether your t-shirts will be available online only or if you'll eventually be aiming to sell in stores. Design a marketing strategy that involves both free and paid advertising methods to expose your brand to your target market. Compose a practical business plan to use as a guideline for operating. For starters, identify your brand's values, mission, objectives, strategies, goals, and long-term vision.

3. Know Your Competition.

You should always be familiar with the other clothing labels you'll be competing with. If you're starting a label based on humorous t-shirts, you should watch what all the other funny t-shirt labels are doing. Keep track of things like their design variety, pricing and promotion, because it may spur some new ideas for your own business strategy. This can be done easily nowadays by reading the blogs of competitor brands and subscribing to their newsletters to keep tabs on what they're up to. This knowledge can help you keep up.

4. Create Products People Would Actually Buy.

It seems obvious, but you'd be surprised at some of the t-shirts you can find these days. Test the quality of your t-shirts by getting honest opinions from others, preferably people who are within your target audience.

5. Know the Finances.

Once you know what you plan on doing, get an idea of how much everything is going to cost you. When you start producing and selling t-shirts, keep track of all of your expenses. Get screen printing quotes from several printers and compare prices to get the best deal, without sacrificing quality. Add in the cost for labeling, hang tagging, bagging, or whatever other finishing options you might use. Don't forget the cost of shipping envelopes, boxes, and product storage.

Don't be fooled by the hundreds of new t-shirt start-ups you see these days; starting a t-shirt business isn't cheap. A lot of the costs involved should also help you decide how much you should charge for your clothing.

6. Come Up With a Promotion Strategy.

Figure out a way to spread the word that makes it easy for those who discover your brand to spread the word to others. For starters, your strategy can include PPC ads, press releases to blogs, and social networking. You can even give away t-shirts with your logo for free. Using guerrilla tactics and promotional items like this can have a tremendous impact on your business growth.

However, don't be a "cheapo." Sooner or later, you'll realize that you're going to have to spend money to market your t-shirt business, so you should be willing to pay for things like online ads, event sponsorships, and other paid marketing methods. Understandably, not everyone is "rollin' in the dough," so find smart ways to balance paid promotion with free promotion to create an excellent strategy.

7. Find Partners.

You might start out on your own, but you should find partners to help maximize your brand's potential and help you reach your goals more efficiently. Aim to have partners within your company while also collaborating with other businesses that may be of some help to you.

8. Set Business Goals.

How many t-shirts do you plan on selling this year? How about this month or this week? A lot of people new to the business have no idea, or just don't care. Then there's the group of people who are too scared to set a goal out of fear that they won't reach it. A successful business sets goals so it has something to aim for.

Set a goal and believe in your ability to reach it. As the law of attraction goes: If you know you're going to reach it, you're going to reach it. If you decide from this day forward that you will sell 10 t-shirts every week, and you strongly believe in your business, you'll do everything you can to figure out a way to get those tees moving. If you don't set a goal, well of course you'll be stuck with a box of t-shirts you were too scared to sell.

9. Don't Quit Because You're Not Seeing Sales the First Day.

That's a good way to get you nowhere. Try to figure out ways of improving your designs, your strategy or your work habits. When you're just getting started, you're still learning, so keep at it. Winners never quit and quitters never win. Read informative, motivational books to keep your spirits up. Frequently visit other brands' websites and blogs, and see how much fun they're having to remind yourself of where you want to be in a few years and how bad you really want it.

Reanalyze your business plan, promotional efforts, and branding strategy. Consider how you compare to the competition and emphasize your competitive edge. Whatever you do, don't quit. Finish what you've started.

10. Have Fun.

If you're in it just to make a quick buck, you're not going to succeed—and that goes for *any* business. Love what you do and do what you love. Your passion will definitely show in your brand image. The more fun it is, the more productive you'll be.

Go Ahead!

The following pages will elaborate on the suggestions provided in the above article and also offer much more. Starting a t-shirt business is a fun and profitable journey, and the abundance of information you will learn here will make it easier. Get ready to kick-start your brand and kick some ass!

3

A SIMPLIFIED STEP-BY-STEP

In order to get to a new destination, you need a map. Consider the following step-by-step plan your map to t-shirt stardom. Actually, since we know all brands don't climb the ladder to success the exact same way, we've drawn out more than one step-by-step plan to give you a broad idea of your forthcoming journey. These are common paths taken by many entrepreneurial brands. Take a look at each one and decide which fits you best.

Plan A.

1) Come up with a brand idea.

2) Develop the idea and decide on a name.

3) Revise the brand idea through multiple developmental stages.

4) Establish a solid brand identity.

5) Develop product ideas based on the brand identity.

6) Produce multiple products to form a collection.

7) Promote your new brand and its new collection before its release.

8) Release the collection to the public online.

9) Escalate promotion of your brand.

10) Media outlets announce your new brand.

11) Your brand develops a fan base and customer base.

12) Continue to promote your brand in any way possible.

13) Whether or not your first collection was a big success, design and produce a new collection within 2-5 months.

14) Repeat steps 7 through 13 as many times as necessary until you begin to catch the attention of retail shops.

15) Create a wholesale catalog displaying all your products along with purchasing information.

16) Send your catalog to potential retailers.

17) Sell your t-shirts to retailers in bulk at wholesale prices.

18) Continue supplying your worldwide fan base through online product sales.

19) Repeat all previous steps until you can afford to exhibit at major clothing trade shows to attract even more retail shops.

20) Open up your own retail shop to sell your products face-to-face with your customer base.

21) Experience an immense increase in revenue as you sell your merchandise through multiple channels.

22) SUCCESS ACHIEVED!

Plan B.

1) Come up with a brand idea.

2) Develop the idea and decide on a name.

3) Revise the brand idea through multiple developmental stages.

4) Establish a solid brand identity.

5) Develop product ideas based on the brand identity.

6) Produce multiple products to form a collection.

7) Promote your new brand and its new collection before its release.

8) Release the collection to the public online.

9) Escalate promotion of your brand.

10) Media outlets announce your new brand.

11) Your brand develops a fan base and customer base.

12) Continue to promote your brand in any way possible.

13) Whether or not your first collection was a big success, design and produce a new collection within 2-5 months.

14) Repeat steps 7 through 13 as many times necessary until you've made enough profit to save several thousands of dollars.

15) Open up a brick-and-mortar retail store to sell your products face-to-face with your customer base.

16) Keep your clothing exclusive to your online shop and retail store, no matter how many other retailers show interest.

17) Experience an immense increase in revenue as you sell your merchandise through your online shop and additional brick-and-mortar stores you open across the country.

18) SUCCESS ACHIEVED!

Pathway To Success

These are just two ways to get to the top, and many have made it via alternate paths as well. Overall, having a good idea of where you're headed and how you're getting there is the best way to start your journey. With these common step-by-step plans in mind, you can begin to think about a more elaborate business plan and figure out your short-term and long-term goals.

4

PLAN EVERYTHING

The planning process may be one of the hardest steps in creating your t-shirt brand, but it is arguably the most essential step to creating a successful business of any kind. As the old saying goes, "If you fail to plan, you plan to fail." The following guidelines can be used as a basis of what to plan and how to plan it effectively.

Setting Goals

A major part of planning for your t-shirt brand is goal-setting. You need to know exactly what you're looking to accomplish with your brand in order to make progress. One of the best methods for setting goals is the *S.M.A.R.T.* method, which stands for:

Specific – The "who," "what," "where," "when" and "why"
Measurable – Can be measured in numbers
Attainable – Realistic; Possible to be reached with effort
Relevant – Resonates with you and inspires you
Time-bound – Has a deadline or time limit

One of the most important aspects of the S.M.A.R.T. goals acronym is the 'R' for Relevant. You have to set goals that are attainable, but which are also relevant or inspirational. For example, a goal of selling two t-shirts in your first month may be easily attainable, but it's completely uninspiring and the payoff is really weak, so you may not be motivated to achieve that. On the other end, setting a goal of 300 t-shirt sales in your first month may be inspiring, but it is most likely an unrealistic target (assuming you're not running a million-dollar promotion campaign or you're not a celebrity).

We can't tell you exactly what your sales goal should be, but if you're just starting out, a sales goal of at least ten t-shirts sold in a month should be both reasonable and inspiring enough. Of course, selling ten t-shirts isn't anything to brag about, but achieving that simple goal should give you the momentum and confidence to sell at least 15 t-shirts the following month, and then 30 t-shirts the month after that. And then after several months of building your brand exposure and reaching previous sales goals, the goal of selling 300 t-shirts in a month will be pretty realistic.

It's good to set product sales goals for your brand, but you also need to consider other goals that may help increase your sales. Here are some questions to consider when setting goals for your business:

1) How many t-shirts do you want to sell this month?

2) How many retail stores do you want your t-shirts to be sold in, and by when?

3) Which trade show or event do you plan on exhibiting at 6 months from now?

4) What magazines do you want your brand featured in 6 months from now?

These four goals should be sufficient to get you started and working in the right direction. Make sure to actually write or type your goals so that they're easier to remember and work toward.

Setting Objectives

So now you're looking at a sheet of paper with a list of your goals. Each of your goals have solid deadlines. You made sure that your goals are S.M.A.R.T.

But wait! How exactly are you going to reach these goals? Setting goals is nice, but it's even nicer to actually reach them. To make sure you reach your goals, you need to map out a plan of action. Take each goal that you set and define the objectives, or "mini-goals," that will help you reach your main goals.

For example, let's say it's currently early June and you've set the goal of selling ten t-shirts in the month of July. Let's also suppose that you haven't ordered any t-shirts yet, but you have already decided on your brand idea, created your designs, and saved up enough money to get your brand started. In this case, your objectives may look something like this:

1) Launch seven products for sale in online shop.

2) Have brand featured on five blogs.

3) Get 100+ daily visitors to website.

Your objectives should be the "meat" of your goal. The objectives you establish should be designed in such a way that completing them will equal reaching your goal. In the beginning, it can be hard to know for sure that completing your objectives will lead to the completion of your goal, but by establishing them, you'll have a clear sense of how to go about reaching that goal.

Setting Daily Tasks

A great way to make sure you stay focused when you're running your brand is to set daily tasks and objectives to complete. Without having clear tasks for the day, you'll end up sitting at your computer for 12 hours, bouncing back and forth between dabbling on some t-shirt design in Photoshop, checking your e-mail, posting links on your friends' Facebook walls, and browsing clothing brand sites. You'll be really busy all day, but at the end of the day you'll realize that you really didn't accomplish much. I've been there and it sucks when that happens.

It's really difficult to concentrate on tasks that you haven't defined beforehand. It's a bad idea to just wake up in the morning, hop on your computer, and "get to work" without having a written checklist of what work you'll actually be doing throughout the day. It's best to define what tasks need to be done each day in order to achieve the goals you set.

After you've set goals and objectives, you need to divide up the objectives into tasks. To make things a bit less complicated, define the first three tasks that need to be done for each of the objectives. So if your objectives were to launch seven products for sale in your shop, get 100+ daily visitors to your site, and have your brand featured on five blogs, your tasks may look like this:

Launch seven products for sale in my shop
- Prepare t-shirt designs into print-ready files
- Request a quote from three screenprinters
- Place an order with one of the screenprinters
- Take photos of products once received
- Upload product shots and info to online shop
- Announce new products to mailing list subscribers

Get 100+ daily visitors to my site
- Search for potential SEO keywords
- Implement SEO on website
- Post an update to Twitter and Facebook daily

Have my brand featured on five blogs
- Create a write-up about my new products
- List 15 blogs that might be interested in my brand
- Contact the 15 blogs to announce my brand

After establishing the tasks for reaching the objectives that will help reach your goal, you should then assign days on which you'll complete each task. Something we do to keep on track with all of our tasks is write them in a daily planner. This makes it easy to break down your tasks into manageable amounts of work each day.

Chaz Matses' Planning Process

Planning ahead is an absolute necessity for creating a t-shirt brand. Jumping into the industry without a plan is a surefire way to ensure that your brand will not be successful. The first step is to make sure that you aren't starting a clothing business for the wrong reasons. Many people think that starting an independent clothing company is an easy way to make quick money. However, this mindset is an incredibly inaccurate representation of the independent fashion industry.

Running a brand requires extremely hard work that won't reveal payoffs until months, sometimes years, down the line. This market has become so polluted and saturated with brands that it takes passion, dedication and time to create a unique identity that sets itself apart from all of its competitors.

In the end, you'll notice that the success of your brand all comes down to one word: passion. Everyone is passionate about something, whether it is baseball or computer programming. Your brand will absolutely not succeed if being a clothing brand owner isn't your passion. So, how do you know if this is really your passion before you've even jotted down notes and ideas? Well, what got you to this point so far? Why are you reading up on starting a t-shirt brand? If you are spending the time to do as much research as possible, then you are on the right track.

Do you buy clothes from other independent companies and think of ways to improve their products? Do you spend night and day thinking about design and name ideas? If so, then creating a detailed business plan for your future brand is the next path to take.

The business plan for your brand is basically going to

be your step-by-step map in the creative process. You want to cover as many things as possible so that you will be better prepared once your plan becomes a reality. I will use my business plan for my brand as a guide for this section.

The first steps I took included writing down hundreds of brand name ideas. Taking the time to pick the perfect brand name can be an extremely long and frustrating process. The method that I used was to write down any words that came to mind when I thought about what I wanted my brand to represent. I had always been a history buff and I wanted to incorporate that passion into my brand.

Some people can find history to be quite boring, however, so my goal was to create a brand name with a contemporary feel that would stand out. After jotting down hundreds of words, I then looked for some outside help. I threw out name ideas to personal friends, family members and to people on t-shirt community websites.

After taking in all of their feedback, I found my final name to be Vicious History. You may not come up with your brand name the way I did, and there's nothing wrong with that. Don't be afraid to test out your ideas on your peers, as getting outside opinions is very important.

The next step I took was listing design ideas and potential artists. Make sure that your design ideas revolve around a central theme that represents your brand. Nothing is worse than releasing your newest collection only to realize that the products don't relate with each other.

Design ideas can be tricky to put into words, so print out pictures and articles that inspire the look you are going for. There are thousands of graphic artists out there, so make sure you do your research and hire the ones who have the style you are looking for (*that is, if you're not creating the designs yourself*).

The next step is to take into account the type of shirts you will be using, and the method of having them printed. Just as with artists, there are loads of blank t-shirt companies, so go with the ones that have your preferred styles, fits, colors and prices. If you aren't printing the shirts yourself (which is most likely the case, unless you're a screen printing specialist), shop around for quotes from screenprinters and decide on the best option based on your business plan.

The last section of the business plan should account for shipping, handling and accessories. Chances are, if you are starting a brand, your start-up capital isn't going to be very much. This can be a bit limiting until your company starts to grow, but always try to put free items, such as fliers and stickers, into your budget. Figuring out your shipping method can be pretty intimidating and confusing at first.

In your business plan, write down your shipping methods step by step until everything looks right. Take into account packaging, scales, shipping supplies and postage methods. Before you launch, it's always good to test your shipping methods by sending a package to yourself or a relative to ensure you won't encounter any problems.

The final section of my business plan included all of the necessary financial information. Planning your costs and expenses is a very important step that you shouldn't overlook. Jumping into a business without doing any sort of financial research will only slow your business down and reveal your lack of professionalism. Request quotes from graphic artists, web designers and apparel companies and incorporate them into your business plan so you can compare prices and make the best decisions for your brand.

I have seen companies in this industry with starting

budgets ranging from several thousands of dollars to only a few hundred dollars. Some of these businesses have succeeded, and others never made it past their first year. Don't worry about other people's budgets or whether or not yours is large enough to compete. Building a successful clothing brand doesn't depend solely on money. It requires countless hours of dedication and passion.

With that being said, don't rush to launch your brand if you can't cover many of the important expenses right off the bat. If you are at that point, spend more time raising the necessary amount of funds before you pull the trigger. The moment you launch your brand, it will be out there for everyone to see, and you don't want to give a poor first impression. It will be easy for consumers to notice that your brand isn't very professional, and that will greatly reduce the chance of them purchasing something from your store.

So much more goes into planning a successful brand than just ideas for cool-looking t-shirts. You need to develop a brand image that encourages the consumer to purchase a product. Having a clean and user-friendly website, professional product photos, high-quality garments and exceptional customer service are just a few of the things that contribute to a powerful brand image.

The most important step to take prior to launching your brand is doing large amounts of research. You can never do enough research for your brand; there is always quality information out there to help build your brand.

Regardless of the amount of research you do or the quality of your business plan, you are going to make mistakes. The mistakes aren't what matter in owning a business; what matters is your ability to recognize and correct them in order to promote continual growth within your company. Having a diehard passion for your brand and learning from experience is what will lead to success within the independent clothing market.

Chaz Matses is the owner of the brand Viscous History (www.ViciousHistory.com)

Don't Get Wrapped Up In Planning

After stressing how important it is to plan, you'll probably go into a planning frenzy, trying to create the perfect plan for your brand to guarantee success. But while total lack of planning can guarantee failure, so can over-planning. It goes along with the phrase "too much of a good thing is bad." Planning your goals, objectives, and daily tasks will put you on the right path, but if you overanalyze your goals, second-guess your objectives, and obsess over perfection when trying to get tasks done, you're not going to get anywhere.

When running our previous t-shirt brand, we used to meet every Sunday and spend three hours planning and evaluating our marketing efforts, creating new objectives, and writing new tasks that we felt would put us closer to our goals. We'd also go as far as projecting sales figures five years into the future and rewriting some of the same objectives and goals that we set last week, since we never accomplished them.

While some of the planning done during these sessions was helpful and served as a guide for our business, much of the planning was just a waste of time and an excuse for inaction. By the end of the month, we'd realize we kept ourselves busy with hours of planning, but no significant progress was made. We actually spent more time planning than executing. Nowadays, we keep planning sessions down to one hour, one day a week.

To avoid getting too wrapped up in planning, it's best to focus on one or two main goals and the objectives surrounding those goals. If you set a goal that may take three years to achieve, break it up into smaller, one-year goals. Even further, break that one-year goal into goals that can be achieved within three months each. It's easier to stay focused on something that can be achieved in three months versus three years.

If there are plenty of tasks you must execute to achieve a certain goal, consider writing only the daily tasks for the current week that will lead to some progress on the set objectives. Then when the next week rolls around, write the tasks for that week.

As obvious as it sounds, it's important that you actually understand your own plan. We used to print out business plan templates from the Internet and fill in the blanks with a bunch of jargon about how we're going to run our business, based on other business plan examples we saw online. While we had several pages full of planning written out, we couldn't really comprehend our own plan. It looked like a professional plan (at least to us), but the only thing it guaranteed was confusion and lack of sufficient action.

It's better to over-act then over-plan. Yes, there are financial risks associated with running a t-shirt brand, and mistakes can have negative effects on your bottom line, but don't be afraid of taking action and making mistakes in the process. You can have the perfect business plan and still fall short of your goals. That's okay. Just review what went wrong and reset your goals and objectives. The point of planning is to provide you with clear direction and focus to make your brand successful.

5

RESEARCH

There's no getting around it. You need to arm yourself with knowledge while developing your brand. It's important for a brand owner to be aware of what is happening in the t-shirt industry in order to maintain an edge over other brand owners and to discover the best way of reaching the customers you want. Here are some of the most important things you should research prior to starting your t-shirt business.

Identify Your Niche Market

Chances are, you're somewhat familiar with the term 'niche.' By definition, a niche is "a place or position suitable or appropriate for a person or thing," "pertains to or is intended for a market niche" or "has specific appeal." In other words, your niche market is a classification of the specific kind of people for whom your t-shirt brand is intended. To simplify this concept, here are some basic examples using fictional t-shirt brands:

The niche market of *Ponies4Ever* would be people who love ponies and horses and who have probably visited a ranch or rode a horse at some point in their lives. *Monsta Truckas* clothing brand might appeal to fans of the monster truck scene.

But neither of these fictional brands would be created to appeal to people outside of their niche, such as the niche market of "tech geeks." There is less of a chance that tech geeks or any other outsiders to the brand's niche would be attracted to the products released by either brand. Now, you might be thinking, "But I want to make t-shirts that anybody would love." This is the classic mistake of trying to please everybody, and it typically won't do you any good. In fact, every successful brand, whether it be in the clothing industry or some other industry, leaves out certain groups of people in their branding and marketing efforts in order to zero in on specific niche markets.

Identifying your niche market is a vital aspect of developing your branding and marketing strategy. Here are easy ways to decide who your t-shirt brand is intended for.

1) Identify different niche markets you would be classified under by listing your interests and hobbies. These niches might be suitable targets for your business.

2) Decide what kind of people you'd want to wear your t-shirts. Rock stars, you say? Your niche market would be rockers and fans of rock music.

3) Think about the kind of people who would find your products valuable or even benefit from them in some way.

Once you have identified your niche market, consider the estimated size of the market in order to determine if it is a profitable niche. Are there enough people in this niche market to keep your business running? Would the people in this niche market even be interested in t-shirts? The town of Beaconsfield, Iowa has a population of 11, making Beaconsfielders one of the worst choices for your niche market. Don't make the mistake of choosing too small of a group.

Availability Of Idea

So you've got a great idea for a t-shirt brand. Maybe you've even designed some t-shirts or went as far as producing a batch of shirts already. Awesome! But hold your horses, buddy. Before getting overly excited about this new idea of yours, you've got to make sure it's not already being used. When developing an idea for your t-shirt brand, research should be a part of the process. Conduct an extensive Google search to make sure that your brilliant idea is also a unique idea. Search a variety of word combinations that could be used to describe your brand to fully ensure that nothing similar exists online.

Look out for any similarities in other clothing brands out on the market. If your brand revolves around a theme, be sure that no other brand presents the exact same theme in the exact same way you planned on presenting it. If another brand is already based around the theme you planned on running with, presenting the theme in a new way will differentiate your brand. For example, one brand might be based on a horror theme while another horror-themed brand presents it in a cute way. Cute zombies.

Availability Of Brand Name

Before choosing to stick with a name, find out if the name is available for use and is not trademarked. You can run a trademark search on the US Patent and Trademark Offices website at **USPTO.gov**. Also check to see if the name is available as a domain (preferably a URL ending in *.com*). This can be done on **GoDaddy.com**. Perform a Google search of the name in quotation marks to see if anything else exists with the same exact name.

If you find out your brand name is being used, it might still be 'available.' You're only banned from using a name if another company using the name is also selling clothing. Although this is the case, it would still be silly to use a name already being used, as this may cause brand confusion, especially if you happen to be targeting the same niche market. Hopefully you haven't already printed 200 t-shirts only to find out that your brand name is already being used by another similar business.

About Your Brand

In some cases, you will have to further educate yourself on the actual content or theme of your brand, as it will make developing ideas easier. For example, if your brand is about cars, it would be a good idea to learn all there is to know about that topic, from the history of the automobile to every car model ever made. This additional knowledge enables you to implement solid branding.

Believe it or not, in some cases you may also have to research the meaning of your brand name. If you make up a word or a name, for example, you should always Google it to make sure it makes sense and is appropriate in all major languages. You don't want to ignorantly make up a name for your brand that you later on find out translates to "urine" in German.

Or maybe your chosen name means something positive to you but ends up being a synonym for something else. One day I came across a really cool clothing brand with awesome branding. They requested a feature on T-Shirt Magazine. To write a comprehensive post, I needed additional pictures of their products, so I did a Google Image search for their brand name. What came up inspired me to write this segment. Their brand name, apparently, was also the name of some rare human deformity that was pretty repulsive to look at. It would suck for their fans to Google their name only to see what I saw. Probably an innocent mistake on their part, but you might want to avoid making that same mistake. Make sure you research your brand name and anything else related to your brand.

Get Feedback

You've got a great t-shirt brand developing in your mind, and it's 100% awesome to the max. Or is it? Do other people think your idea is awesome too? And we're not talking about your mommy and your best friend Mark. You've got to get other people's opinions on your ideas—people who don't know you, because they couldn't care less about hurting your feelings. You need to hear the truth about your idea before going too far with it. We've all seen bad ideas taken too far.

Feedback is important, not only for beginning your t-shirt business, but for maintaining it as well. Be ready for all kinds of feedback, and use your judgement to decide what to listen to. Ask for feedback from associates, co-workers and even strangers. Simply proposing the question *"What do you think of the name (insert brand name here)?"* can give you a good idea of where your brand name stands upon first impression.

Watch Other Brands

Pay close attention to brands that inspire you. You can take it even further by researching everything about them: how they started, how they are maintained, the ways they are marketed, where their t-shirts are sold, and anything else you can manage to find. You can gain inspiration and learn a lot from your favorite brand. Discovering how they built up their business can give you ideas and motivation to build yours. Successful brands can also serve as good models for your own brand.

Other Things To Research

Beyond the basics, some things to consider looking into are industry trade shows and craft fairs, which you might be interested in attending to get a preview of what lies ahead for you and your business. You also want to research the costs involved in launching your t-shirt brand (some of which will be explained in the next chapter).

Karlo Reyes' Research Process and Brand Progress

In today's street culture movement, it's difficult to know which brands are relevant when it comes to the concept and meaning behind each one of them. Jeepney is well known for its bold graphics and edgy concepts in the streetwear market.

However, most people don't realize that the concept behind the brand has deep artistic roots (Jeepney Trucks) and cultural (Filipino) relevance which inspires its designs and overall brand strategy.

At first glance, it's not easy to make the connection between a Jeepney and fashion. That's why I wanted people to know why I chose the name and why it's relevant to everyone that wears the product.

When I chose a name for the company, it was important that the name was not only unique, but artistically and culturally meaningful. To me, a Jeepney embraces the artistic element of street culture simply because as artists we all want to showcase our talents in a unique way for the world to see. The most unique feature of the Jeepney is that each vehicle is different in design and concept. What were once plain American GI Jeeps left over in the Philippines after World War II have since been transformed into urban art forms that showcase each owner's individual style.

As for the cultural relevance, at the end of the day, if all of our customers are able to look fly and learn a little about the Filipino culture through the Jeepney brand, then we feel like we accomplished some sort of educational purpose— even if it takes edgy graphics in our designs to get it done.

I am a graphic designer by trade and had a graphic/web design company back in the day. I started Jeepney in 2003 when I did a few t-shirts for a community festival. I ended up selling out of all the tees, so I decided to keep doing it. I brought on my business partners—Rex Korrell late in '03 to help with the operations and the sales side; David Gavino for design help; and Simpson Wong as the CFO—and the rest is history.

When we first started, there wasn't a lot of information

available on how to create a t-shirt brand, so we basically made things up as we went. We also asked our screenprinters for a lot of advice. Fortunately, we found a mentor, Mel Matsui, who was a seasoned veteran in the apparel industry to guide us with the basics of the industry.

From there, we created an online store, sold at events, and visited **MAGIC** (the largest apparel wholesale show in the US). Then, in 2005, we did the **POOL Tradeshow** in Vegas and the **Agenda Tradeshow** in San Diego, which exposed our brand to the large mainstream stores. From there, we started exhibiting at MAGIC, and everything just snowballed and we had a full-time business. We got into stores like **Karmaloop**, **Metro Park**, **Urban Outfitters** and many Japanese and European stores. We also did a lot of important collaborations, which brought the brand tons of exposure.

Over the years, I have been involved with plenty of other brands and have seen companies start from scratch and go on to sell in the multi-millions. The main steps I would say are:

1) Know how you will stand out from the rest of the other brands out there.

2) Have a clear idea of who your customer is and why they would choose your brand as opposed to the thousands of other t-shirt brands in the world.

3) Create a business plan. It doesn't have to be super complicated, but you need some sort of guide for your vision, your mission and your goals. If you don't have a clear vision of where you want your company to be in one, three or five years, then you will just be spending money and time with no real direction.

You can start with a few thousand dollars, but in my experience, to really create a functional brand and be able to sell to large stores, the tipping point is to do tradeshows like MAGIC and Agenda and basically hang with the big boys. For this, you will need at least $50,000. This can take a long time, which is fine, and this should in no way discourage anyone, but it should be the monetary goal for someone starting up. This will help with production costs, marketing, overhead and a small amount to be able to pay a part-time employee. If you budget correctly, that should last you about a year.

If you don't have the capital, you can factor it with a finance company. Basically they will pay for your invoices for a certain percentage of your POs (purchase orders).

Create an online store and learn how to use social networking sites to market your brand. Exhibit at as many trade shows as you can. The more frequently buyers see your product, the more they will recognize you. It takes time, so don't be discouraged if you don't get a lot of sales the first few seasons.

As corny as it sounds, don't give up. You will face many hurdles, but if you keep at it, somehow things just happen. So if you want it bad enough, you will make it in the industry.

Lastly, have fun with your company and don't let the daily grind make you forget why you have this business in the first place. Think of the business as a "game," and play the game to win. You can create the "rules" or use other people's rules and change them to fit your company. When you can view it from that perspective, it makes the whole thing a lot more fun and enjoyable.

Karlo Reyes is the founder of Jeepney.
(www.JeepneyClothing.com)

6

CREATING A SOLID BRAND

Often times when people think about a t-shirt brand the first thing that comes to mind is the company's logo and some of its t-shirt designs. Although those are elements of the brand, there's more to it than a logo and designs. Your brand is the whole experience your customers get when they buy your products. A solid brand will have long-lasting effects on the success of your business.

More Than Just T-Shirts

Consumers often buy products out of habit, because they become loyal to the brands that produce them. It's more than likely that there are a few brands that have been in your house for the past 10 years, because you or your family have become loyal to those brands and continue to buy their products. That's not to say that the brands you've become loyal to are necessarily better than all the rest. They just happened to grab your attention and keep it long enough to build a relationship with you as a buyer. You want your t-shirt brand to do the same to members of your target market.

Your t-shirt brand is more than just a collection of t-shirts. Your 'brand' is the personality of your entire business. Your 'brand' must evoke emotions and create sensory experiences while exhibiting admirable human qualities. Everything from the t-shirt designs and packaging to the website and marketing, and even how you answer emails and phone calls, plays into the essence of your brand. Your brand personality should be unique to your business. It is what distinguishes you from the rest of the t-shirt businesses out there.

What Do You Stand For?

First and foremost, in order to begin creating a solid brand, you need to stand for something. What, or who, does your brand represent? The things you stand for form the foundation around which your brand should be built.

In addition to standing for something, your brand must offer a unique selling point. What do you offer that other brands don't? What is so special about your brand that would pique people's interest? What do you promise that others don't, or can't? Your unique selling point should answer all or some of these questions. If you have done your research and have already come up with an original idea for a t-shirt brand, this step becomes easy. Your original idea is one of the unique selling points that sets the foundation for your brand personality.

Everything you do with your brand should be in line with your unique selling point, either directly or indirectly, otherwise you risk losing the impression you intended to make on your customers. If your unique selling point is that you offer the most dirt-cheap, high-end t-shirts, you've got to stick to that. You can't decide to shift your prices suddenly to increase your profit margin or to afford better-quality fabrics. If your unique selling point is that your t-shirt designs broadcast the biggest current events, you've got to be in tune with the latest controversy, perhaps even keeping your customers up to date through your blog.

Maintaining your brand image by being true to your unique selling point is the key to building a solid brand. Here's an illustrated example of the importance of this.

A hypothetical brand, 'Eco Catz,' promises eco-friendly, feline-inspired t-shirts made in the U.S.. If Eco Catz were ever to release even *one* t-shirt that was made in China or that wasn't environmentally friendly, there would be an outrage from their loyal customers. Even if it was discovered that the Eco Catz headquarters doesn't practice recycling, their whole reputation could be at risk. Therefore, the people at Eco Catz know that, based on their unique selling point, they must continue to produce their clothing in the United States of America, be feline-inspired, and be as eco-friendly as they claim to be. Customer loyalty depends on it.

Your Brand Name

Just as important as your unique selling point and what your brand stands for is your brand name. In the previous chapter we covered this briefly, but there's more to a brand name than its availability. Your brand name should be strong, likable and memorable. It should be easy to pronounce, and most of all, it should reflect what your brand is about. A good brand name is suggestive of your unique selling point but is not too narrow that it decreases your ability to claim new selling points in the future.

A name like 'Awesome Black Tees,' for example, restricts a brand to producing just black t-shirts. Anything else would be out of line with the brand identity, since right off the bat the name establishes that the t-shirts will be black. It's no wonder most big-name brands refrain from ending their brand name with the name of a specific product. Notice it's not *Tide Detergent*, *Nike Sneakers* or *Hanes Underwear*. They are simply *Tide, Nike* and *Hanes*, allowing them to sell more than just detergent, sneakers and underwear.

Too many new t-shirt brands make the mistake of adding "apparel," "threads," "tees" or a similar word to the end of their brand name, and it really limits their potential expansion. If fact, we made this mistake with our previous brand. The name suggested t-shirts and t-shirts only. Just imagine how awkward it would be if we had decided down the line to produce jeans or footwear under a brand name with the word "t-shirt" in it.

Your Brand "Profile"

Describing your brand properly is a necessary skill for building a successful clothing line. After you've pondered a bit about your brand and what you stand for, you'll have to create a brand "profile," which will be very useful on your forthcoming journey. Not only does your brand profile help clarify what your company is all about, it also shows that the people behind the brand are knowledgeable about what they're selling and know how to present a great idea.

Your brand profile should be included on your website, within your catalogs, and in press releases. In many cases, it's your one shot at reeling in your target customer. Just look at it as a dating ad for your brand. You want to attract as many potential "dates," or customers, as possible, so you want a profile that speaks to members of your target market. Some people have trouble describing their brand in words, and if you're one of those people, don't lose sleep over it. It's often hard to put into words exactly what your brand is about. Let's work on getting that down.

When writing your brand profile, what you're aiming for is to convince your target customers that your brand is exactly what they're looking for. If your products aren't giving people a solid idea of what your brand is about, the "About" page on your website (where your profile should be located) is your only hope.

It helps to be pretty specific about what your brand means rather than establishing yourself as a generic t-shirt brand. I've seen tons of new t-shirt brands that I didn't really understand right off the bat, but which I got a better understanding and appreciation for once I read their brand profile. I've also seen profiles by new brands that have a negative impact on the brand's identity. It automatically makes me pass over the brand and look for something better.

If you don't want to be overlooked, follow the guidelines mentioned in the previous **What Do You Stand For?** section and answer the additional questions below:

What does your brand name mean and how does it relate to your products?

What kind of theme is prominent in your designs?

What words can you use to describe your products?

What are some notable features about your t-shirts?

If you can tackle those questions, you can write a great brand profile. Try to avoid cliches like claiming your brand is "unique" and "something new."

That kind of nonsense is what we call fillers. Fillers are what amateur brand owners use to describe their new brand when they don't really know what the hell their brand is actually about. None of this stuff will have a great impact on whether or not a potential customer will consider buying your items. Instead, focus on describing *what* makes your brand so unique and cool rather than simply *claiming* to be unique and cool.

Don't make vague, heroic statements like "We're here to take the clothing industry to the next level" or "We're going to change the t-shirt game forever!" These are just more nonsensical fillers. That kind of talk is nothing but your company's generalized goals—goals which many other brands also have. It doesn't increase your chances of gaining new customers.

Don't flood your brand description with unnecessary information about yourself or your team. Things like "We always wanted a clothing line and finally our dreams have come true" or "We each have our own unique styles and ideas." That kind of personal biographical data is of no interest to the potential consumer and teaches them nothing about your brand. You should only mention things about yourself that actually relate to the brand identity.

For example, if your brand is composed of fishing-themed t-shirts, it's okay to mention that you've been a fisherman all your life. That kind of information actually adds to the brand experience. On the other hand, knowing that you and your best friend Steve have been trying to sell tees for the past three years doesn't help in highlighting the brand itself. This will sting a little, but customers don't care about you. At least not until you've proven yourself through your brand identity.

Your Brand's Visual Identity

After establishing your unique selling point and brand name, use them as a guide for creating your brand's visual identity: the look and feel of your brand. When you think of a brand, one of the first things that comes to mind is the way their products look, as well as any colors or graphics associated with them. A brand's visual identity is the primary feature consumers recognize it by. The look and feel of your brand can be inspired by a number of other things, such as your own aesthetic taste and what you feel best communicates the theme of your brand.

The main components of your brand's visual identity include the logo, the color scheme, the fonts and the images. Each of these components should be presented frequently and consistently. They should also go hand-in-hand and nicely complement each other. Unity amongst the visual aspects of your brand's identity is key. Imbalances in your brands visual identity can have a bigger impact on your target market than you might think.

To illustrate the importance, imagine a fictional t-shirt brand, 'Gothicality,' whose brand identity is as Gothic as you could imagine. Gothicality fans are hardcore Goths who love the whole Gothic culture. Most people would imagine an overall dark color scheme, Gothic font styles, and graphics such as crosses, pentagrams or skulls. But imagine Gothicality printing a design with big pink hearts on a yellow t-shirt. That would be totally incongruent and the product probably wouldn't sell. The same would be the case if any aspect of your visual brand identity didn't match.

To ensure complementary visuals, work on unifying the following key aspects of visual brand identity:

1) Logos
2) Colors
3) Fonts

4) Images

Your visual brand identity will be the first thing consumers recognize you by, so it's essential that it is congruent with your overall branding and reflects your brand image well. It is also a pivotal aspect of developing your brand.

Ha Mai's Story and Brand Development Process

Fur Face Boy is an outlet where I can be myself as much as I possibly can. It's an extension of my own personality: quirky, strange and random as hell, yet full of raw emotion and heart. By trade, I'm a graphic designer, so I'd like to think that I kinda know how to make things look good, flow well and be presented well.

When I first started Fur Face Boy, the main purpose was to just have an outlet where I could creatively do what I wanted to do, how I wanted to do it, and when I wanted to do it, without anybody telling me otherwise. At the job I was working at previously, I was the lowly graphic/production designer under three directors (art, creative and marketing)! I was tired of always having to take orders from others and having my ideas and input valued with so little regard!

My favorite pieces of art and design have always been the pieces I did on my own time. The joy that you get from the freedom to do things your way is unbeatable! I've always wanted to mess around and experiment with t-shirt printing and starting a t-shirt line so I figured "Yea, I'm going to try this." I didn't plan on being 'the next big thing'; I just wanted to give something that I was interested in a shot. It's as simple as that.

One day, I was rapidly flipping through channels on my TV, one after another after another after another, but I was highly intrigued when I saw a TLC special on the 'Wolf Boy,' a boy who lived in India that had hair growing all over his face! I figured, if I was so intrigued with this 'Wolf Boy,' then I wonder how people would react if I made a graphic of him and printed it on a shirt? So that's when I thought, "What the hell, why not?" and I had the perfect quirky, strange and random name for my brand: Fur Face Boy!

I started Fur Face Boy with two designs: the original face logo on a white shirt, and a typeface logo on a black shirt. I printed about 75 or so of each design. Yet after I had all of these shirts printed, *no one* was buying them. My family and friends weren't sold on my brand, but I didn't care, I was having fun and I loved the challenge of proving that I could make this happen, all via passion and love! But since no one was buying my shirts, I then thought, "Man, forget this. I'm just going to start giving away these shirts for free!"

I then started a blog with the very little knowledge I had of Macromedia Dreamweaver, and I started a Myspace page as well. It was through these two web outlets that I began taking names and addresses down from random people all across the nation so I could send them a FREE Fur Face Boy tee! My goal was to get at least one shirt in each state.

The trade-off was that the person who got a free shirt simply email me back with a photo of themselves wearing the shirt, which I then posted on my blog (I let them know, of course). People love being seen on TV and on websites! It excited them to the point that they went and told their friends about my blog, and I slowly got more visits. Aside from a few sales, 95% of the first run of Fur Face Boy shirts were given away for free. That's how I built brand awareness and how I created buzz. To this day, I still do contests and random giveaways!

Eventually, after a few months, I had about six to ten other designs, and I opened my web store. Slowly I got sales from my web store from people who were taking notice of my brand.

Aside from online sales, I knew I needed even more exposure, so that's when I decided to create special box sets to ship out to specific stores that I envisioned seeing my tees in. These box sets came with a sample of the shirts, the shirts' bells and whistles, and all of the quality and small details my brand had to offer.

Everyone wants to feel wanted, so that's when I decided to personalize each box set. These box sets got these shops' attention to the point that they welcomed my tees to be sold at their shops. And with this, my brand got even more exposure! Now people could pick up my shirts via my web store or at these certain brick-and-mortar shops.

I also sent these sets to bloggers, newspapers, magazines, radio stations—anywhere, really—just to get a chance for more exposure. Sure I wasn't making money right off the bat, but I knew that publicity and exposure are vital when first starting a business. Presenting yourself and being memorable is key to being recognized.

I also do many events and try to work with people and store owners around my area to build a community around my tees. Sell some tees, have some food and drinks, and hear some great music. I make it fun and try to talk to everyone who comes out to such an event. I want them to build memories and have fun, so they associate these positive feelings with my brand.

Along with my blog, web store and presence in certain boutique shops from California to Texas, I picked up my social media game. Twitter, Facebook, Tumblr, Blogger as well as T-Shirt Magazine are all important aspects to keeping your brand fresh and new. It's fun and it gets your customers involved! People love knowing that there is a real person on the other side willing to interact!

With these social media sites, you can continue to make your brand buzz! As for my blog, people love visiting to read about my life: where I go, what I do, what I eat, what I wear, and what I think are all part of my brand. Like I said earlier, this brand is an extension of me and my personality. It's hard to believe, but my life and the way I live is what sells the brand. The shirts have become secondary!

As for the shirts, they are what represent the entirety of my brand. So it's a no-brainer to make sure that my products are top-notch through and through. I make sure my designs are executed on point and are extremely polished. I'm such a perfectionist when it comes to my designs that I would probably burn all of my tees if I overlooked something that had already been printed. The labels, the small details like the packaging, the "inspected by" stickers and the hang tags— everything must be perfect!

All tees are limited because no one wants what everyone else has, especially when it comes to clothing! Also, every aspect of a Fur Face Boy tee is 100% made and produced in the USA. It's small details like these that will help your brand be more appreciated and noticed. But it will definitely take time.

All in all, I just live life. I get inspired by the things and places I visit and see, the people I meet, the music and movies I see and hear, the books I read, the websites I visit, and the food I eat. I am inspired by everything! And when you're open-minded and can appreciate the things around you, inspiration will constantly hit you. I also work hard and try to accomplish something related to my brand every single day. Whether these accomplishments are big or small, I work towards making results.

Be sure to have fun! Don't be so serious. Don't think too hard! Just be spontaneous and go with the flow. Sure, I worry before all events, but at the end of the day, I'm still breathing. And one last very important rule: Use common sense! If you need to find the answer to something, it's most likely right in front of your face! Ever heard of Google.com? You can find pretty much any resource you need there!

Put in some work! Don't wait around for a hand out. Make things happen on your own and you will see how rewarding it's going to be! Each progressive move you make will help you transition to your next move, and your next, and next.

Ha Mai is the founder of Fur Face Boy
(www.FurFaceBoy.com)

7

LEGALITIES

When preparing to launch a t-shirt brand, it's important to know the legal aspects involved. If you're anything like us, the legal aspects are probably something that you aren't all that interested in handling. But going to jail, getting sued, or getting our ideas stolen is something that we're even less interested in handling. With that in mind, it's better to understand the legal matters before launching your brand to help guide your decisions while you're running it.

Disclaimer

The information provided in this chapter is believed to be accurate at the time of this writing. This information is based on our research and our experiences running a t-shirt brand and should serve as a general guideline. Since we aren't attorneys, we suggest that you consult with an attorney as well as a CPA for further legal and tax advice.

Copyright and Trademarks

A **copyright** gives the copyright holder the right to be credited for the work, to determine who may adapt the work to other forms, financially benefit from it, and other related rights. A **trademark** is a type of intellectual property—typically a name, word, phrase, logo, symbol, or a combination of these elements.

You should copyright your t-shirt designs and trademark your brand name and logo to protect them legally. But don't stress about copyright and trademark too early; legal protection is not necessary to *start* your t-shirt business (but is recommended if the funds are available). It's definitely necessary as you progress, however. ***LegalZoom.com*** is a great service for obtaining trademarks and copyrights at an affordable price. Including all associated fees, we got our brand name trademarked for around $600.

In fact, when we first started ***Cashletes***, we didn't have a trademark for the brand name. But I realized that we were better off spending our money on developing the brand rather than on legal protection. Also, considering our history going from business to business, brand to brand, I figured that if we had gotten all of those past brand names trademarked, we would have lost a whole lot of money since we never profited much from those projects.

The way I look at it, in the beginning stages of your development, it's unlikely that someone would try to "steal your ideas," as many new business owners fear. Especially since your idea hasn't become profitable yet. If you were someone who went around stealing business ideas and brand names, why would you steal one that hasn't proved to be profitable yet? But once we developed Cashletes to the point that it was profitable, we immediately applied for legal protection.

Also, here's a quick tip for the early unprotected stages. Put the ™ symbol on your logo anywhere it is shown or printed. That way people would assume that your brand name is trademarked, even if it isn't. I don't know about you, but I've never second-guessed whether a brand name was legally protected if it had a ™, © or ® on it.

T-Shirt Design Legalities

When it comes to creating your t-shirt designs, you might be inspired and influenced by other images, ideas and people out there, but be careful where you get your inspiration from and how you go about creating your designs based on that inspiration. In some cases, borrowing ideas and images may be fine, but in other cases, you can get into trouble doing so. We'll make sure to clarify the t-shirt design legalities for you.

Images from the Internet

Images from the Internet are usually protected by copyright unless they're from a non-photographer's photo album or something. There's also a new search feature on the website *CreativeCommons.org* that brings up search results of images that are free to use under the Creative Commons License. Among the search results, you can choose to view images that you can use for commercial purposes, or images that you can modify, build on, or adapt.

There are ways of beating the traditional copyright system though: If you use a basic, generic picture—for example, one of a dog—you'd probably get away with it in some cases. If there is nothing peculiar about the photo you use and it looks like something you could very well have photographed yourself, most likely the copyright holder won't really be able to distinguish the image. On the other hand, if you use a picture that's very specific or complex—for example, a picture of a white pitbull with black spots wearing a football helmet and eating M&Ms—you could get caught easily.

Using Famous Quotes

When using quotes in t-shirt designs, you should give credit to the person who originally said the quote rather than pretending that you made it up yourself. Credit the speaker either on the design itself, on the hang-tag or label, or in the product description.

Using Popular Characters

Never use popular cartoon characters in t-shirt designs unless you have a license to do so. Just make up your own characters or get someone else to design characters for you. Simple as that. Using popular characters in an attempt to sell quick is just plain crooked and uncreative.

Parodying Popular Figures and Icons

It is, however, okay to parody popular characters and figures, thanks to the *Right to Parody*. Just don't get too crazy with it. When your parodying becomes overly offensive, you may get attacked and/or kidnapped by the entourage or fans of the figure you're parodying. Or maybe even nabbed for defamation of character. Just beware.

Political Figures

In most cases, political figures can be used in your t-shirt designs. It's no wonder there are so many political t-shirts on the market. The only situation you wouldn't be safe using them is if you find a famous photo of a political figure. The photo would most likely be recognized as the photographer's famous photo, so you'd be in hot water.

Kind of like when Shepard Fairey was in trouble for using a famous Obama photo to create his widely popular "Hope" poster. In addition to political figures, you can also use flags, coats of arms, and national symbols wherever and whenever you want.

Writing and Signing Contracts

Contracts may come into play when working with new partners or forming new alliances. When signing a contract, read it thoroughly, at least twice. And don't sign a contract for anything until you've thoroughly considered the consequences of agreeing to what it entails, as well as how you'd feel about your decision to sign when a few months go by. Find some sample contracts online or in books so you get an idea of how they should be formatted if you plan on creating your own.

Business Entities

Another important legal aspect in regards to launching your t-shirt brand is the business legal structure you choose. You can run your business as one of the following:

1) Sole Proprietorship

2) Partnership
3) Limited Liability Company (LLC)
4) Limited Liability Partnership (LLP)
5) Corporation

To cut to the chase, we would suggest that you establish your t-shirt business as a Limited Liability Company. To quote **LegalZoom.com**, the reason an LLC is a good option is because:

"They combine the personal liability protection of a corporation with the tax benefits and simplicity of a partnership. In other words, the owners (or members) of an LLC are not personally liable for its debts and liabilities but also have the benefit of being taxed only once on their profits. Moreover, LLCs are more flexible and require less ongoing paperwork than an S corporation."

Just to clarify, the reason we chose to establish our business as an LLC is because we wanted to have our business set up as a separate entity, or a "fictitious person," so that we are able to open a bank account under the business name. We also wanted to have protection of our personal assets (personal cash, houses, cars, or any other personal possessions that hold value) so that down the line, if our business is involved in a legal dispute or gets into debt for some reason, our personal assets are safe. Furthermore, we didn't want to deal with the complications involved with corporate bureaucracy, yet we were still able to establish ourselves as a 'credible' business.

It's not necessary to establish a business entity before starting your brand, but if you have more than enough funds on hand to get your products produced and your brand marketed, it would be a good idea to do so.

Just to give you an idea, It cost us about $800 to establish our business structure. However, if you don't have enough money to form an LLC, we would recommend that you at least legally get a

DBA (Doing Business As) for your business, since it costs less than forming an LLC.

In other words, with a DBA, your business would be considered a sole proprietorship (if you're the sole owner of the business) or a partnership (if multiple people own the business together), and you'd be able to open a bank account for your business. By getting a DBA for your business, you'd get some of the benefits of forming an LLC, but without the same legal protection (your personal assets won't be protected). We'd recommend changing your business structure to an LLC as soon as you're able to.

The point of this section isn't to go deep into explaining the legal jargon, since we're not legal experts, and this book isn't about business law. It's more of a short guide highlighting what you should be aware of, since legal issues do come into play when running a t-shirt brand. Prices for business formation and registration will vary depending on the state you're filing your business under and the legal services you use.

For more information on the different legal structures, check out LegalZoom's *Business Formation Comparison Chart*: **www.legalzoom.com/business-formations/compare-documents.html**

8

FINANCES

Starting a t-shirt business could cost you anywhere from $300 to $10,000, or even more. It all depends on the size of your collection and the quality or complexity of your individual products. And don't forget about the cost of marketing and any other add-on expenses, such as packaging. In addition, it's important to be aware of the reoccurring costs of running your t-shirt business.

To give you an idea of what to expect as far as costs go, we'll break down the costs of the typical start-up brand and outline a few other notable financial aspects.

Know The Finances

These costs are to be used as examples only; they do not reflect the expenses of every t-shirt brand out there, and they may not perfectly reflect the expenses of your brand, either.

Hypothetical Start-Up Expenses:

Six different designs screen printed on 24 shirts each **= $1,152** (*at $8 per shirt, 144 shirts total*)

Three colors per shirt design, so 18 screens used in total **= $270** (*at $15 per screen*)

144 Woven labels **= $80**

Labels sewn on all 144 shirts **= $180**

144 Polybags **= $20**

144 Mailers **= $30**

Charges for everything shipped to you **= $70**

An e-commerce website, designed and hosted **= $1,000**

Total= $2,802

As a general rule, you should expect to invest an initial amount of at least $1,000 to launch your t-shirt business to get the best results. You could of course decide to go the cheaper route and put out maybe two or three t-shirts and call it a collection, but chances are you will reap what you sow and have mediocre results.

You're better off saving up the money for a complete line of t-shirts, because it will have a more positive effect on your overall strategy and payoff in the long-run.

For start-up costs more specific to your business, continue reading. We explain more in the chapter on product production.

How We Got Funding

A big hurdle for most people who are looking to start a t-shirt brand, once they are aware of the finances, is actually getting the money to start their brand. Usually, those who want to start a t-shirt brand are young people with an average to below-average income determined to make money doing something they love.

When we started our clothing brands, we didn't have jobs or enough money saved up to fund a successful start-up. When we created our first clothing brand we had about $350 saved up from selling ad space on T-Shirt Magazine, but we needed much more funding, so we asked our dad for $1,000.

We actually went as far as creating a detailed funding proposal stating how we planned on using the money, how much money we were expecting to make from the sales of our t-shirts, and our marketing plan. We did a whole presentation on it, as if we were asking an investor or a bank for a loan. Even though he had "blind faith" in us, we still felt that it would be necessary to approach him as if he were a big-time investor. After hearing our presentation, he decided to give us the money we needed to launch our brand.

As we stated in the introduction, despite a good start with our first brand, sales started to decline month after month, and we ran out of money. Our parents didn't have any more money to give us either, so we weren't sure how we were going to rebuild our brand. We were still determined to run a successful t-shirt brand, so we started over in a totally different direction with Cashletes.

After the crash of our first t-shirt brand, we made sure to craft the Cashletes brand so that it would run successfully. We made sure to carefully plan how the funds would be used and back up our financial income and expense projections with real calculations rather than making guesses.

Luckily, when we were launching the first collection of Cashletes, our dad was able to give us another $1,500 to get started. We were able to produce some t-shirts with this funding and start selling again. We were off to an okay start, but we realized that we couldn't keep asking daddy for money to run our business, nor did he have a lot of money to just shell out whenever we needed it. So we took matters into our own hands.

Since we were skilled at graphic design, we decided that we could raise money to fund our brand by offering graphic design services to other upcoming brands. A month after our brand launch, we started promoting our services as graphic designers on the Internet to earn extra income. Our graphic design business took off, and we were able to raise enough money to invest in our t-shirt brand and fund it properly to propel it to success.

We continued to invest money from our design services to boost production, and eventually our t-shirt brand became sustainable on its own and we no longer needed to add outside funding to promote sales.

How You Can Get Funding

What usually comes to mind when people think of getting funding for their business is taking out a bank loan or maxing out credit cards. The problem with this is that in order to get a bank loan for your business, you typically have to have a detailed business plan that includes a cash-flow statement of your business from the past two to three years. That's basically a 'catch-22' situation. How can you have a cash-flow statement from the past two to three years to start a business that you haven't even been running for two to three months?

Also, as far as maxing out credit cards is concerned, you may be in for a whole lot of debt if your t-shirt sales don't come in the way you had planned. And if you have bad credit history, or no credit history at all (like when we started), then maxing out credit cards isn't even an option.

So instead of going the traditional route when it comes to getting funding, we'd recommend a more 'realistic' approach to getting the money you need to launch your brand. If you're in a position to get a sufficient bank loan or to use your credit cards as funding, then the following tips might not apply to you. But if your situation is anything like ours was, then this is the perfect approach.

Ask Your Relatives

This is what we did when we first started, although reluctantly. We felt we had to do it if we wanted to launch a clothing line. Sometimes asking your mom or dad for money is the last thing you want to do, especially since you don't want them to think of you as a dependent little kid. But if you know exactly how you're going to use the requested funds and are aware of what it takes to run a t-shirt brand, you should be able to convince your relatives. After reading several start-up stories, we realized that a few other successful businesses have started with investments from relatives, too.

I'd suggest that you take it seriously when approaching your parents or extended relatives for start-up cash. When asking your relatives for a few thousand dollars, give concrete reasons why they should invest in your new business, backed by a detailed plan of action that their investment would make possible.

Just like we did when starting our brand, create a clear proposal stating the amount of money you need, as well as details on how that money will be used and how you will earn that money back through your sales. But don't complicate things in your plan of action. It doesn't need to be a 50-page traditional business plan. What's important is that you have a few pages stating the essential details of the funding you need to produce your t-shirts. Also include other associated costs such as promotional efforts and website building. Your plan for selling your products and a basic strategy for reinvesting the money you'll make is also necessary in your proposal.

Remember, if you're *borrowing* money from your family members, you should make it clear that you will *return* their investment, possibly even with interest added. However, when adding interest, you don't want to set an extreme return on investment, such as borrowing $5,000 to launch your brand and saying that you can give them $5,000 + $1,000 interest within two months. It would be very difficult to accomplish something like that, and you'd be misleading the investor.

Instead, set up fair terms for yourself and the person you're borrowing the money from. Possibly a 12-24 month return period would be a more reasonable term. When we borrowed money from our parents, we didn't have any terms for return on investment, but we did eventually pay them back the initial investment and much more.

In some cases, your relatives might give you money without a convincing proposal or a promise of return on their investment, just to support your dreams. Either way, you must make it clear that they are only *investing* in your business and that you aren't asking them to become your new business partner, unless that's your intention. Making the funding and operation terms clear from the beginning when asking for money from family can help prevent misunderstandings later on.

Ask Your Friends

If your relatives don't have the spare cash to lend you for starting your brand, consider asking a friend. If you already have friends who are professionals or have a stable income, consider proposing your need for funding to them. When we were starting out, this didn't really seem like a viable option, since most of our friends were either just out of high school or still in college, just as broke as we were.

Your situation may be different, though, especially if you're a little bit older than we were when starting and have friends who have already started careers. Try making a list of five to ten friends who might be able to lend you the start-up money that you'll need. Maybe your friend John who works for that advertising agency might be interested in investing in your idea. Perhaps your friend Sara who started a pretty successful jewelery line has enough money that she'd be willing to invest in your brand. You should aim to ask optimistic and positive friends who are likely to encourage your entrepreneurial pursuits.

But just like you'd do with family members, make sure that you present the need for funding in a serious manner, providing clear terms and your plan of action. Again, you don't need a complicated plan; just a straight-to-the-point document stating how you'll use the financial contribution and make the money back.

When asking your friend for funding, he might take an interest in becoming part of your business and getting a percentage of the sales revenue from your business. If you really don't like the idea of having that particular person as a partner, don't agree to those terms. However, if you decide to bring a partner on board who's providing funding, make sure that the rules regarding ownership and decision-making power are clear from the start.

For example, if you want this friend to be more like a "silent partner" who doesn't have any control over your t-shirt business in any way but receives a certain percentage of your business income every month, make sure to have that clearly stated in your written proposal for funding and restate it when you're talking with this person. Write out a contract between the two of you so everyone is on the same terms.

Nobody Willing to Lend

In some cases, you might be faced with rejection, harsh criticism, or be completely taken as a joke when asking friends and family for money to start your t-shirt brand. Some of them may really believe in your ideas but simply do not want to risk investing their hard-earned money into your business. Others may completely refuse to give you any money to get started simply because they don't believe that you can make real profit selling t-shirts online. Some may ask you why you're even starting a clothing brand in the first place and try to discourage you altogether.

When it seems like you're running into walls asking your friends and family for funding, it's time to consider other alternatives.

Start-Up Funding Sites

Another option for getting start-up cash is to ask the people of the world wide web. Sites such as *KickStarter.com* and *CrowdFunder.co.uk* serve as funding platforms for creative projects. People looking for funding for their projects simply create an account and create an in-depth funding proposal. The projects people post on these sites range from producing a movie to creating a line of vinyl figures.

You'll also find many proposals for launching a clothing collection, some of which have successfully received the necessary funding to become a reality. You can ask for donations of just $5 or up to $2,000, but you must give those who are donating something in return. One of the benefits of these fundraising platforms is that you don't have to reciprocate their money; instead, you offer the donors another kind of incentive, such as the t-shirts you print or recognition on your site as a contributor.

Enter Design Contests

If you're a skilled artist or graphic designer, consider creating designs to submit to contest websites. Some of these websites give out prizes of $2,000 or even as high as $20,000 for bigger contests. The most popular ongoing t-shirt design contest out there are hosted by *Threadless.com* and *DesignByHumans.com*.

If you do a Google search for 't-shirt design contests,' you'll find a whole bunch of sites where you can submit your designs for a chance at prize money. There are also other contest sites, like *CrowdSpring.com*, on which you can enter an unlimited amount of mini graphic-design contests for a chance to win money.

I'd suggest doing this only if you already frequently create artwork for fun. It can take a while to win one of these design contests, but if you have the skill and dedication to create cool designs on a regular basis, you may eventually win and obtain the funding you need to get your t-shirt brand started.

Start a Side Business

Being artists all our lives, we knew that we had the talent required to make money using our skills. We designed t-shirts and websites for our own businesses, so we figured we could design for other brands, too. If you possess the same talents, consider setting up an online portfolio of the work you've done and start soliciting your services.

You can directly contact companies who you think might benefit from your services, or you can let your friends know about your design services and see if they could suggest you to potential clients. Also, you can apply some of the tips we'll mention in the "Marketing Your Brand" chapter to market your design services online.

Another great way to get exposure as a graphic designer is to get listed or featured on a site with visitors who might be interested in your services. For example, *NextDayFlyers.com*, a site that provides printing services for filers, business cards and other promotional materials, has a section in which they feature graphic designers. Since people who visit this site need to get promo materials printed, it's likely they'd also be interested in graphic design services for their promo materials, which means they are looking for the services that you provide.

Not a graphic designer or artist? Maybe you're a skateboarder looking to start a skate brand, but you're not exactly talented at creating t-shirt designs. Why not give skateboarding lessons to people trying to learn how to skateboard? Maybe you've been practicing drums all your life. How about offering lessons in that? Basically, if you have a skill you can teach that people would be willing to pay for, then it's worth giving it a try to earn some extra money. It doesn't even have to be a "skill"—any service you can offer will do, for instance, freelance writing or even babysitting.

You can save the money you make doing freelance work or from your side business to invest into your brand. You can decide to discontinue your side business once you launch your brand.

Save Money From Your Current Job

If you're already making a living from your current job, consider setting up a plan to save enough money to launch your brand. Try to live off of slightly less then you earn. We can't tell you exactly how much you should put aside to save up for your business, but see if you can manage to save at least 10% of each paycheck you receive. The amount you save per week can determine how quickly you'll be able to attain the necessary funding for your brand.

Decide on an estimated date for the projected launch of your brand, and then count back two months to calculate the date by which you will need to begin the production of your products. In other words, if you want to launch your brand by June, you should start production in April.

Then decide on how much funding you'll need to get started, and divide that amount by the number of weeks until the day you plan on making initial payments for funding your brand production. Let's say the initial cost for funding your brand is $2,000, and you plan on launching in five months (20 weeks). In this example, you'll have to begin production in three months (12 weeks). So you'll need to have saved up $2,000 in 12 weeks. Knowing this information allows you to split up the total amount needed and figure out that you will have to save $167 per week in order to accumulate the necessary start-up funds.

Get a Short-Term Job for Extra Cash

If you currently can't think of any skills you can utilize as a freelancer, can't save enough from your current job and don't have family or friends to ask for money, getting a short-term part-time job might be the solution. Make sure it's something that will be at least slightly appealing to you. You don't want to be stuck mopping floors at McDonald's for a few months, unless that's your idea of a good time.

Consider signing up for several mini-jobs here and there, like helping set up a concert, being a summer camp instructor for a few weeks, or posing as a model for an art class. These kind of paid "gigs" won't require a long-term commitment, and by doing enough of these you may be able to collect enough money to get your brand off the ground.

Have a Garage Sale

Another funding option to consider is to sell a bunch of stuff that you don't need anymore. You can do yourself a favor and put your selling skills to the test by having a garage sale. With the help of your friends and family, you can gather a bunch of items such as clothes, toys, books, furniture, and other things that you don't need anymore, and set up a garage sale to sell them. You can even promote your garage sale around the neighborhood.

All of that junk sitting around your house just might earn you the money you need to invest in your clothing brand. You can even opt for the modern-day garage sale, also known as *eBay.com*. Put some of your old trash up on the site for others to discover as new treasures.

9

DESIGNING T-SHIRTS

Now it's time to get to the heart of the matter: designing your t-shirts. This chapter helps you get started on your t-shirt designs, explains how to keep the creative process flowing smoothly, and offers tips and advice to help you get past some of the obstacles every brand owner faces.

What Makes A Kick-Ass Design

Quite simply, a good t-shirt design is one that sells like hot cakes, and a bad t-shirt design is one that sits on the shelf for years without a sale. Until you get into the swing of designing and producing t-shirts, it can be hard to figure out a formula for creating what could be considered a 'good' t-shirt design. Sometimes, when designing a collection of t-shirts, we'll have a certain design that we consider the best. Our opinion doesn't always prove to be true, however, and that 'best' design of ours sometimes ends up not doing as well as we thought it would, compared to the other designs.

Although this topic can be debated endlessly, a good design can be defined as one that succeeds at communicating its intended message or theme while being aesthetically pleasing to the intended audience. If you can create designs that do this, then you're off to a good start. At the end of the day, it's not you but your customers who decide what makes a good design. You will just gradually get an understanding of what works and what doesn't.

Getting Started

After doing your research and laying down the foundation for your brand, ideas for t-shirt designs should come naturally. Often times, t-shirt design ideas come before you even consider anything else, so it's likely that you have hundreds of ideas running through your head already. Based on the visual brand identity you've planned out, begin to think about what will be the prominent look and feel of your t-shirt designs. Not all your designs have to look exactly the same, but the overall essence of the line should be similar, or there should be some reoccurring theme or symbol present. Some new brands ignore this simple fact and end up creating a collection that looks like more than one clothing brand.

Start off with a few sketches to bring your ideas to paper. You can print out a line drawing of a t-shirt to use as a template, or simply draw a t-shirt outline yourself. Even if you won't be finalizing your designs for print (that is, if you plan on getting a designer to create your designs), it's still a good idea to sketch out what you envision so that your designer has something to go by. But we'll get to outsourcing design work later. At the earliest stages, developing your ideas is most important.

Pre-Name Your Designs

A good tactic for developing a t-shirt design is coming up with possible names for the design while creating it. You don't have to stick with that name once all is said and done, but having a rough idea of a possible title is great for developing a design. This gives you a more grounded concept of the design and also prevents the challenge of having to come up with a name for a miscellaneous design after it's completed.

This brings us to a similar concern: originality. Just like your overall brand concept, each individual t-shirt design should also be original. Thanks to Google, you can confirm the originality of your designs. If you've thought about some possible titles for your designs, you can easily type those, or related keyword phrases, into the search engine.

Pre-Plan The Production

During the idea development stage, it also helps to think about the types of t-shirts and production processes you will use to produce your designs. For example, will the design be an all-over print or a small chest print? Will it be screen printed or embroidered? Will there be any additional print locations, such as the back of the shirt or the sleeve?

You should answer these questions and more while developing your ideas rather than saving them as afterthoughts. Equally important is the issue of design colors. Keep in mind that more colors usually means higher production costs. If you plan on getting your t-shirts screen printed, you will most likely get charged per color on each design, in addition to a one-time screen charge for each color.

The Collection As A Whole

While developing your t-shirt designs, try to think of each idea or design as a part of a collection. Refrain from creating a collection that is all over the place; each t-shirt should flow into the next. If you've planned out your brand personality correctly, creating a flowing collection should be no problem. Maintaining a reoccurring theme or style is the easiest way to do this.

A line of t-shirts is similar to an artist's portfolio. Having an artist's background and going through multiple art schools, it was always stressed that your portfolio should be in sync, even though you may use different media depending on the assignment given. The same applies to your t-shirt collection. Although you might incorporate different styles into each design, there should always be a common ground.

Even something as simple as color scheme is a way to keep the collection in sync. How about making all your tees black and white? Or maybe entirely neon colors? Whatever you decide on to unify your t-shirts, make sure to keep it consistent for the first few releases.

We'll often have someone ask us, "Well how about such and such brand? Their t-shirts don't look the same. You can't even tell what their brand is about." We used to think the same thing, but we soon realized that many of those brands actually *did* start off with a solid theme for each collection. They've just expanded to the point that they've already established the direction of their brand and are thus able to take on new themes and looks while maintaining their customer base. Once you've proven yourself as an outstanding brand, you can literally do whatever you want and your customers will still throw money at you. Just look at some of the big-name brands on the store racks.

Kyle Crawford On Developing T-Shirt Designs

The process from which I get my ideas is pretty complicated yet easy. The explanation is almost A.D.D.-ish. Sometimes an idea just comes to me and sparks a ton of other ideas. In previous lines and upcoming lines, I usually come up with a phrase or a saying that will map out the entire line.

For instance, in Fall 2009, I had two phrases that pretty much paved the way in terms of branding. There was *"Taking Over The World Since 2007"* and *"The Streets Are Ours."* Both are phrases I still try to incorporate into ideas and designs. There's just so much you can do with it. It paints a picture for an entire line.

Last fall, it was *"Destroy Everything."* That gave me so many ideas. I try and paint a picture from both sides (in this case, from the perspective of a zombie and from the perspective of someone running for their life). It works both ways. *"Kill or be Killed," "Streets."* I'm pretty proud that I was able to come up with something on a whim that basically set a foundation for ideas, when in fact I don't have any ideas at all.

I can think back and go, "Okay, I've got this really good phrase, what can I do with this? Alright, take two iconic characters from previous shirts and have them battling in a city." That particular idea came from the phrase *"The Streets are Ours."* I even put the zombie in the original *"Kill or be Killed"* shirt.

A lot of the time, I look over a line after it's done, and an idea will come into mind. Sometimes I look at a design and immediately see what I could do to make it better. I also feel like you can never have too many ideas. I think sometimes people only focus on the "right now." I always try and come up with more designs than I need.

You never know, if something does well, you won't have to worry about how you're going to top the last line. You've already got a head start.

I think with my day-to-day work designing for bands, I get really fortunate with ideas, even though bands don't always give me direction. For instance, the *Pentagram* logo and design idea was sparked when I was designing for **Alkaline Trio**. I stopped what I was doing for them and started toying with how I could incorporate my brand into a pentagram. I'm still really impressed with how it turned out.

Other times, I'll be doing a design for a band and as I'm working along, I think to myself, "This would be a great design for Electric Zombie." There are even times when I don't finish the design and just save it for months later when I start working on the next line. I write everything in a book of ideas. I think it's really important for everyone to have one. Or at least a note pad on a computer. Some people don't realize that anything that they have going on can spark an idea. It's important to be able to have something to put thoughts (or, in my case, random words) down on. There's going to come a time where you'll need to look back.

It's really important to keep a record. Not everyone is a

machine! That's part of the reason why I also hire other designers. Plus, I like to see what other people can do with my ideas. When I hire out, I am really specific with my concepts and briefs and what I want. I pinpoint exactly who I want working on what, because I know what people's strong suits are and what they're capable of. I think that's really important for people who own a line. There are people who are good at everything, and then there are people who are really good at a particular thing but not so good at another. It's important to keep track of those attributes in a designer.

The main key for me is to be extremely on top of things. Extremely detail-oriented. Maybe get in people's business a bit. You really have to keep tabs on everything if you want to do something new and unique, something that no one has done before. Sometimes you might look at someone else's idea of, let's say, a shirt with a skull, and something about it it might trigger an idea of a hamburger shirt.

There have been times when I didn't have any ideas until the very last second. Sometimes I look back at ideas I wrote and think "What the hell was I thinking?" I still save those kind of ideas though, because you never know! I'm not one of those brands who looks at this as a cash cow or a way to make some money. This is basically my passion that has blown up from a once-small hobby. I just try and make shirts that really suit my personality. I know I'm not the only dork out there who saw the same movies and had the same toys.

I might not be the best talker or the best at customer service, but I try my hardest to put forth as much effort and time as I can to make my imagination come to life. There are so many people who ride the coattails of current trends or who watch like hawks the kinds of things other brands are doing. Some brands have been doing the same thing since the first day they started. With me, I'm just being me. If a shirt doesn't sell off the bat, it eventually will. Or someone will be happy to get a shirt for dirt cheap.

It shouldn't be about money. All you have to do is ask yourself, "What would I like to wear that hasn't been created yet? What hasn't been done before? How crazy can I get? How many faces can I make light up because I basically just took something from their childhood closet and put it on a t-shirt?"

I think the biggest challenge for me is to take a well-known idea and come up with something that will get just as much love and respect but is completely original. Coming up with a theme, or even a color scheme, can really make a difference.

There's just so much that goes on in my head that makes the magic happen. I wish I could fully explain it. Just be completely honest with yourself. Really sit down and think. Anyone can whip up designs with no meaning, anyone can go onto t-shirt sites and forums and buy designs and put their name on it. If you take the time to sit down and think, even one idea can make a line. One phrase, one name, one image. As long as you put the thought into it and do a little research and give yourself some time, and have patience, anything is possible.

Kyle Crawford is creator of the brand Electric Zombie
(www.TheElectricZombie.com)

How Many Tees Make A Collection?

A good range consists of four to ten t-shirts. As you progress, your collection will most likely be even greater, but four to ten is perfect for starting out. If start-up funding is tight, which is understandable, four to six designs are just as good as seven to ten. As long as every design is top-notch, you're off to an excellent start.

Tools Of The Trade

After sketching out some ideas, decide which ones to go with. Getting people's opinions is helpful at this point so that you can make any necessary modifications to your chosen designs before finalizing everything. Upon choosing a design to start off with, decide on the tools and methods you will use to create the final version. Some t-shirt designers create polished hand drawings finished off with ink, while others go straight to the computer to render a design.

Whatever your method of choice may be, here are some useful tools:

- Pencils of varying shades and erasers
- Black markers or black ink and a brush
- **Adobe Illustrator**, Adobe **Photoshop**, or similar software

Once you've finalized your drawing on paper, you make your way to to the most important piece of equipment you will ever need: your computer. No matter how your design starts off, it should be finished on the computer screen. A computer art program such as **Illustrator** or **Photoshop** is necessary for digitally inking and coloring your new masterpiece and preparing it for printing. There is also an amazing free online image-editing software available at **Pixlr.com**. You can easily buy or find the right software online or in stores, but in the case that you have no access to these programs or find it too difficult to use them, you can outsource the work to a designer. We'll talk more about outsourcing work in the "Managing Your Business" chapter.

Beyond finalizing the t-shirt design, these programs can also be used to separate each color in the design into it's own layer. This is necessary for creating screens if you will be screen printing your t-shirts, which is the recommended process. That will be covered shortly.

Creating Kick-Ass Designs

When rendering your t-shirt design in a digital art computer program, be sure to keep it neat and crisp. For starters, I'd recommend canvas dimensions of at least 12 inches in width by 15 inches in height and a resolution of 300dpi. The width and height can vary based on the size and shape of your design, but the 300dpi setting is most important when creating designs for print, no matter what width and height you decide to go with. These settings ensure that your design is high-resolution ("hi-res").

In addition to being high-resolution, your design better be high quality. Take as much time as you need creating your designs. Don't rush a single click, and don't stop until you're completely satisfied with the outcome of your work (or, if you happen to be an unsatisfiable critic when it comes to your own work, at least until other people agree that your design is finished).

Getting Unbiased Opinions

Before you go and print a thousand t-shirts, it helps to get feedback on your designs. To get an idea of what others think of your new designs, post them online and wait for responses. A good website to post on is ***Mintees.com***, which has a whole community of dedicated t-shirt designers who will gladly give you feedback.

You can also submit your design to a t-shirt contest website like ***Threadless.com***—not with the intention to win, but to see what the response is like. If you do happen to win, you'll get some start-up funds out of the deal, but you'll have to hand over the rights to the design to the contest site, so you won't be able to use that particular design for your own brand.

In this age of social networking, you can also post your designs on ***Facebook*** or any other social-networking site to get feedback from your friends and random people. Just upload a design to Facebook and see if anybody "Likes" it. If nobody out of your 1,653 friends and pseudo-friends "Likes" a particular design, that should tell you something. You can also post your designs in the online forums you regularly visit.

Revise and Edit

This can't be stressed enough. Always revise and edit your work until you're completely satisfied with it. Any time you create a t-shirt design, it's okay to be obsessed with making it perfect. This isn't just a class project or side hobby anymore—it's your business, a business you plan on making money off of. If anything is important, it's quality.

Production-Ready

After you've created a design, you'll have to prepare it for production. For designs you will be screen printing, separate each color in the design into a separate layer. Each color layer is its own shape, which is then burned into screens which will be used during the transference of ink to your t-shirts. Save the file as a .PSD (Photoshop file), .AI (Illustrator file), or whatever file type the screenprinter needs. When preparing a file for digital printing, the required file type is usually a JPEG (or JPG).

You can also provide your screenprinter with a Pantone color guide of each color to be used in each design. This helps assure that the exact colors you want used in each design are the colors that get transferred to the final product. Besides color accuracy, one of the most important aspects of transferring a design to a t-shirt is size accuracy. Whenever preparing files for print, always make sure the dimensions of the file are the exact same dimensions of the design as you want it to appear on the final product.

Or You Can Hire A Designer

The other option to designing t-shirts for your brand is to hire an artist to bring your t-shirt ideas into fruition. If you're not that good of an artist, or if your design style isn't exactly what you envision for your brand, this would be your best bet. The best place to find some great designers is **Mintees.com**, which is pretty much a t-shirt designer showcase. There's an endless supply of talent ready to help you create anything you might imagine.

You can also find a designer by contacting your favorite indie t-shirt brand. See if the designer would be able to create some designs for your brand. Having a popular designer on board could greatly benefit your brand identity. Always be picky when choosing a designer. Find a designer whose work you love and who you confidently feel can help you create some rad t-shirt designs.

Find a quality designer that fits in your budget. Here's a heads up: The typical t-shirt design may cost you $200 to $600 (or more) depending on the complexity of the design and the talent or experience of the designer. Remember to factor those costs into your initial start-up budget.

You can also check out t-shirt design contest sites like **Threadless.com** and **DesignByHumans.com**. These sites hold weekly t-shirt design contests comprised of work by great designers. A lot of these guys never manage to snatch the prize money, but they have work worth rewarding. Browse the members of these sites and handpick the ones you like, then contact them to propose a deal.

Mock It Up

After you've created all of the designs, you should always create "mockups" of each t-shirt. A mockup is a digitally rendered image of what your t-shirt will look like when printed. Find a blank t-shirt template online and create a mockup for each t-shirt in your collection to see what the collection would look like as a whole. Or if you hire a designer, ask him or her for mockups. In many cases, your screenprinter will require mockups before printing your shirts to make sure they have a good idea of what you need done, especially in the case of multiple print locations on one shirt.

A mockup also gives you a more realistic impression of each shirt. A design may look good in your head as you develop the idea and also as you create and prepare it for print but then look totally off when you mock it up. This is simply because some things just don't look right on a t-shirt, or the execution of your initial idea caused it to change. Early on, you may run into this problem, but it's an easy issue to overcome the more you design t-shirts.

10

PRODUCING
T-SHIRTS

You've worked your magic and your t-shirt designs are all ready to go. Now you'll need to get your awesome t-shirts manufactured. There are several different print and application processes to choose from and an endless number of manufacturers who can offer exactly what you need. To produce your t-shirts the way you want them and to have them ready for sale when you want them, you'll have to play an active part in the production process while planning strategically.

A Word On Money

We'll be honest here. Producing products fit to sell is not a cheap person's business. As we've mentioned previously, your t-shirt brand will require quite an investment, but if you work wisely, it's all worth it. In order to create t-shirts of high quality and value, you will have to dish out a few extra bucks. We learned that early on, and it helped us make the decision to leave Cafe Press and Spreadshirt behind.

And if you really want this, you'll figure out ways to raise funds for setting up your t-shirt business the way you envision. Never take the cheap approach unless you'd be content with mediocre results. Also know that most companies you will be dealing with in the production stage will request payment on 50/50 terms: Fifty percent down, fifty percent after the production is complete. This is great because you don't have to make the full payment in order to get things started.

Get It Done Right

At this point, you should have a good idea of exactly how you want your finished products to look. You've created the designs and decided on the styles and colors of shirts they will be printed on. You might even know the exact application process you will be using to get the finished design onto the shirts. Good job. Although you will be handing the rest of the job over to the manufacturers, your task now is to make sure production goes as planned. You've got to be on top of your game now.

Design Application

There are numerous ways to get your designs onto t-shirts, but we're just going to outline the ones we'd recommend. Some processes just wont cut it if you really want your brand to succeed. Iron-ons and fabric markers are perfect examples. Processes like those may pass if you're creating tees as a hobby or selling to friends and family only, but for a successful professional t-shirt brand you'll have to produce products using better methods. It's important that your finished products look worthy of a store rack, and this is best achieved through the professional printing and application processes outlined below.

Screen Printing

Most of the t-shirts you see out in stores or online are screen-printed. This is the main choice for producing professional-quality t-shirts, and it's quite evident why. Screen printing, which is also known as silk-screening, is a printing technique that uses a woven mesh to support an ink-blocking stencil, which is shaped to your design. The attached stencil leaves open areas of mesh through which ink is transferred as a sharp-edged image onto your t-shirt, resulting in a design that is bold and crisp.

There are many different options when it comes to screen printing:

Plastisol Inks – The most commonly used inks for screen printing, made of PVC with an oil base for flow and viscosity.

Metallic Inks – For that shiny metal look, with a subtle, unfinished sheen, you can get your designs printed with metallic inks.

Glitter Inks – Similar to metallic inks, but with glittery specks all throughout.

Glow-In-The-Dark Inks – These inks glow in the dark, as the name suggests, usually in the typical greenish glow characteristic of glow-in-the-dark objects.

High-Density Inks – Can be used to create a print that stands up to 1/8 inch above the fabric's surface, which results in a 3D print.

Heat Transfers

In the case that a design requires an application or texture that isn't made up of ink, heat transfers are used. The heat transfer process involves the application of a design or logo to a t-shirt by transferring the design from a specially printed paper to the fabric by means of heat or pressure. The Do-It-Yourself iron-on sheets you can find at a craft store are an example of heat transfers (but these are for hobbyists and are not the recommended option for professional brand owners).

There are a number of options for heat transferring designs:

Flock Transfers – These transfers have a smooth, fuzzy feel to them, somewhat similar to suede.

Foil Transfers – As the name suggests, these are shiny transfers made of foil.

Other Applications

Dye Sublimation – A printing technique that allows all-over-printing of full-color images with superior softness.

Embroidery – Needlework is used to apply a design in stitched strands of thread.

Patchwork – Combining fabric cutouts and embroidery to create a design.

Stones, Glitter, or Studs – Adding these 3D shiny elements can be done through heat press or adhesives.

Choosing An Application

With all the different design application options, it could be difficult to decide which option is best for your t-shirts. The application we would highly recommend for any brand is **standard screen printing with plastisol inks**. However, based on the types of consumers you're targeting, you may choose to opt for a fancier print application. A t-shirt brand targeting little girls might benefit from printing designs with glitter inks, for example.

A good way to figure out which application methods would be most appropriate for your brand is to browse through your competitors' t-shirts on store racks and online. This should tell you what your target market prefers.

Choosing A Printer

With the plethora of t-shirt production companies out there, it can be hard to decide which to go with. The best approach is to first decide which services you'll need. If you need screen printing (which is the most common), make sure the company offers that. Your friend's dad might have a heat press machine and offer to print your shirts, but if you specifically want screen-printed designs, which we highly recommend, you should turn down the offer.

If you do need heat-pressed designs, however, make sure the company offers that. Typically a company will specialize in one or the other (screen printing or heat press). Other services you may have to consider are label sewing, hang tagging, and bagging. Not every company offers those.

But besides all that, one of the most important things to look for is examples of the company's previous work. Do they have a portfolio on their website? Can they send you a sample of a past print job? Have they produced t-shirts for some brands you recognize? Do they print t-shirts for clothing brands at all or do they usually work with non-profit organizations and schools? All of these are important things to consider that will help you make your decision. A recommendation from a fellow brand owner can also be really helpful. The following t-shirt printers are ones that we can recommend:

Antilogy (AntilogyDesign.com)
Jak Prints (JakPrints.com)
Merch Spin (MerchSpin.com)

David Murray's Advice on Working With Screenprinters

Everyone agrees that having quality products and shipping them out in a timely fashion is important, so choosing the right screenprinter to work with should be one of your top priorities.

Unless, for some reason, you *are* a screenprinter – a *professional* screenprinter, working in an actual shop – don't print your own tees. I could go on and on, but just don't waste your time. Screen printing has a steep learning curve, the equipment is expensive, and no customer wants to pay you to learn how to make a decent print.

Don't bother with friends who have a screen printing machine set up in their garage who are going to give you a great deal, because you will get what you pay for. I can say this because I started off printing t-shirts in my basement, but it wasn't until I started working in a professional shop that I learned how poorly I'd really been printing all along.

Get to know your printers. They're going to be an important part of your business, so do your research. Start looking around online, ask people you trust, or crack open the phonebook (if you actually have one) and start checking out local printers. Make some appointments, meet some of the crew, and see some samples of what they can do. Don't rush to find a printer; take time to do the legwork so you can be confident that you've made the right choice.

Get to know your inks. This isn't absolutely required, but it always helps to do a little research into different types of ink, how they work with various garments, and how the wonders of science will affect your final product. Knowing your plastisol from your pigmented discharge can only help, and your printers should be more than happy to tell you all about the different options.

Ask about contract printing to save money. When a screenprinter buys the tees for your job themselves, they mark them up a bit to reflect the fact that they're putting money in up front. To save some money, if you have an actual wholesale connection (as in, you're a legitimate business that has a wholesale account with a t-shirt distributor), you can buy the tees yourself, have them sent to the shop, and then only pay the printers for the cost of printing. When meeting with a new printer, ask if they do contract printing; in the long run, saving this extra buck or two per shirt will make a huge difference.

Plan ahead. This is common sense, but ideally you want to put in your orders with time to spare (most shops have a one- to two-week turnaround). Having worked in a few print shops myself, I can tell you that the work orders come in fast and the print queue is usually planned out at least a week in advance, sometimes even further during the busy summer months.

Save yourself and your printers the stress and just get your orders in as early as you reasonably can. If you need to change the quantities on an order, that's usually not the biggest deal—just be sure to get that order in. I've been that guy, pleading with his printers to get an order done ASAP. It's not a good look. Sometimes emergencies are unavoidable and accidents happen, but there's no excuse for simply not putting the work in on time.

**David Murray is the creator of Seibei
(www.Seibei.com)**

Choosing A T-Shirt Blank

We're going to cut to the chase here. After reading multiple reviews throughout the development of our brands, there are only two kinds of t-shirt blanks we can recommend. The **American Apparel** kind (aka AA) and the **Alstyle** kind (aka AAA). American Apparel's blanks are buttery-soft, light-weight and fitted. Alstyle's are more durable, fit slightly larger, and sometimes come with tear-away tags. Both of these brands offer a wide variety of colors and styles, too.

The best blank to choose will depend on your target market (or your budget). If your brand is streetwear, urban wear, or athletic wear, Alstyle would be perfect. Otherwise, American Apparel does the job. Cost-wise, American Apparel is more expensive than Alstyle, but could be worth it.

If for some reason your screenprinter doesn't offer these, other notable blanks are **Alternative Apparel**, **Anvil** and **Tutlex**.

Whatever you do, don't just go with the cheapest blanks you can find, just because they were the cheapest blanks you could find. Always go for quality over price. For a good t-shirt blanks review, check out Chazzy Matse's article on T-ShirtMagazine.com entitled "Picking the Perfect T-Shirt Blank."

But the absolute best way to decide on a t-shirt blank is by feeling one firsthand. Request a sample of a few different blank brands you're thinking about choosing, and compare them. Feel the fabric, try the shirt on, throw it in the washer and dryer. A personal trial period beats any review you can read.

After you've decided which t-shirt blank you'd like to go with, you have two options. You can place a wholesale order for the t-shirts online via one of the many websites that sell wholesale t-shirts, or you can have your printer order for you.

Cut-n-Sew T-Shirts

An alternative to getting your t-shirts printed on pre-made t-shirt blanks is getting them printed on t-shirts that are custom made from scratch, specifically for you. This can be done through garment manufacturers that specialize in t-shirt construction. Custom-producing t-shirts requires more initial funds than using t-shirt blanks, and it also takes more time, but the end product is catered to your liking. Every major clothing brand produces t-shirts this way, and you might also want to consider this option eventually.

To find manufacturers that offer cut-n-sew t-shirts, search global trade sites, like *Alibaba.com*, which list a plethora of suppliers and manufacturers for an endless variety of products. When choosing a t-shirt manufacturer, look for important details such as their capabilities, the minimum order quantity they accept, and their cost per unit. Alibaba.com also lets you instant-chat with each supplier, so you can get all the information you need within one chat session.

As with ordering pre-made t-shirt blanks, it's best practice to request a sample t-shirt before going through with custom t-shirt production. Get in touch with at least two different suppliers and purchase samples from them to compare quality. In some cases, a supplier will offer a sample of a past job for free first, and then later make a custom sample for you for a specified cost.

When contracting a custom sample, send the manufacturer a "blueprint" for creating your t-shirt. Include every little detail, from the fabric weight to the exact measurement of the ribbing on the collar. And be sure to supply specific measurements for each shirt size you will be ordering. This will ensure that you get the exact product you intend on creating. You can also send a physical sample of a t-shirt you want yours based on.

Many garment manufacturers also offer screen printing. If you find one that does, you should consider getting your tees constructed and printed by them to save time and money. Just make sure the printing quality is top-notch. Request a sample of a previous print job to see their work firsthand.

After sampling, you'll be ready to place a bulk order of t-shirts. The exact order quantity will vary based on the supplier you choose, but typically the minimums start at 100 tees per color. The pricing might be around $3 per shirt, depending on the supplier. Remember to factor in shipping costs as well. If you only contracted the construction of the t-shirts and not the printing, you'll send your custom-created t-shirt blanks to your printer to complete the job.

Choosing Shirt Sizes

An often overlooked aspect of the t-shirt production process is deciding how many of which shirt sizes to offer. This actually comes down to your customer base, and as you go along, making this decision will become easier. For your first batch of tees, you won't have any customers to base your size breakdown on, but you can think in practical terms.

Firstly, your target market, as well as the quantity of your initial order of t-shirts, would determine the variety of sizes you should offer. The target market only comes into play if there is a distinct size difference between the physique of your intended customer and the general public. For example, if your target customers are college football players, offering more XXXL tees and less small tees would make sense. The quantity of shirts you order is more often the deciding factor, however, especially when your intended customers aren't peculiar in size.

If you order a moderate batch of tees per design (24, for example), don't worry about trying to offer every size imaginable. The basic sizes to offer are small, medium, large, XL, and XXL. As you would imagine, most people fit into a medium or a large, so order more of those sizes. This is based on personal experience as well as on what I've heard from others.

In the order of most to least, demand for shirt sizes is as follows: large, medium, small, XL, and XXL. Another good approach is to get an even number of each size. That way, each size starts off on an even plane and your customers can then decide which sizes they prefer. Always adjust accordingly. If you're ordering a quantity larger than 24, you can add other sizes into the mix, such as XS and up to 4X.

Labeling

When branding your clothing line, it's necessary to show your logo as much as reasonably possible, and it's also necessary to inform your customers about the fabric care details of the t-shirt they will be wearing. The label of your t-shirt is home to all this useful information. It's actually illegal to not have some sort of label on your t-shirt.

The typical label includes the shirt size, the country the shirt was made in, and the fabric care instructions. Other optional items are your brand's logo, an interesting tag line or funny phrase, and your website. Labels can be either woven and sewn onto the inside (or outside) of the shirt, or printed on the inside of the shirt by your screenprinter.

We've always preferred woven labels, since they give a more legit impression. If you plan on getting your t-shirts custom-made, the manufacturer will typically offer woven labeling as well, in which case you wouldn't need to find another company to produce woven labels. If you're printing on t-shirt blanks, you'll have to get the woven labels made elsewhere, as most t-shirt printers only offer printed labels.

When looking for a label supplier, you might run into companies with high minimum quantities and costly unit prices or setup fees, and you might get the impression that you can't afford woven labels. We thought the same thing initially, but eventually we found some affordable options. To give you a head start, here are a few good custom label producing shops.

Laven Industries (Laven.com)
NW Tag (NWTag.com)
Clothing Labels 4 U (ClothingLabels4u.com)

Keeping Up With The Production

As your products are being made, be sure to remain in contact with your suppliers to ensure that things go smoothly. Before getting a printer or manufacturer started on your t-shirts, ask for an estimated time of arrival, and make it your duty to keep tabs on the timeline of the production. After all, the supplier couldn't care less when you get your tees, but you know how important timing can be for your business.

Email your suppliers at least once a week requesting a progress update. In the case of custom-manufactured t-shirts, request photo updates, too. See to it that production goes as planned.

Packaging

A major factor in the t-shirt selling business is presentation, and packaging is all about presentation. To attract buyers and keep 'em coming back, it's essential that you get this presentation thing down and impress the hell out of your customers and potential buyers. That being said, impressive presentation of your t-shirts upon delivery is something to consider. Here's why.

Standing out amongst the competition and going above and beyond are essential components to an effective marketing strategy. When you take a look at some of your favorite brands—of t-shirts and other products alike—it is highly likely that at one point or another, creative packaging was used.

Not many upcoming brands take packaging into consideration, so you will distinguish yourself by doing so. Most just use generic plastic bags or whatever mailer their product will fit in. But it's no surprise that few new brands use unusual packaging or customization to set their product apart. It's simply overlooked.

Cool t-shirt packaging is sure to make a lasting impression on your customers and have them promote your brand themselves through word of mouth, online, and by wearing your merchandise. Examples of great packaging are *Linty Fresh, Johnny Cupcakes* and *410 BC*. For instance, Johnny Cupcakes t-shirts came packaged in cake-mix boxes that were designed to match each t-shirt that came in them, a feature that fits the theme of his company. Be creative when coming up with packaging for your t-shirts.

Let's take a look at the most basic t-shirt packaging options available to you:

- Plastic mailers
- Tyvek mailers
- Corrugated boxes

In the beginning, you might have no choice but to opt for the most basic, least expensive t-shirt packaging options. This is fully understandable, as not every start-up t-shirt business has thousands of dollars at their disposal for unique packaging. But you should at least have plans to improve your t-shirt packaging, along with the rest of your branding, as your budget increases.

At the very least, every t-shirt you sell deserves to be packaged in a plastic poly bag and sent out in a tyvek or plastic mailer. You can get a thousand poly bags on **Uline.com** for cheap and an unlimited supply of tyvek mailers from **USPS.com** for free, so there should be no excuse here. However, this ultra-basic packaging method should only be used if you're really on a shoestring budget after getting your products produced. But eventually you'll want to upgrade to the creative stuff, such as the examples that follow.

Some packaging ideas you may find useful:
- Colored or metallic poly mailer
- Poly mailer with printed design or a logo sticker on it
- Corrugated box mailer with your logo on it
- Wooden box printed or engraved with your logo
- Plastic box or mailing tube with logo sticker
- Tin can or other custom shape

Look around at your favorite brands and brands you consider your competition to see what their t-shirt packaging is like so you can keep up with them. In addition to the exterior packaging, don't forget the items that go inside of the package, such as hang tags, free stickers, posters, postcards and other freebies. You can get stickers printed for a low cost at *123stickers.com*. For postcards and any other printing, we recommend *NextDayFlyers.com*. You can also make hang tags yourself by printing them as business cards and punching ⅛" holes into them (then attach them to your products using a tagging gun). Use your creativity to come up with additional affordable packaging ideas.

Some awesome ideas for inspiration:

- Die-cut custom-shaped hang tags
- Stickers or posters to match the t-shirt designs
- Knickknacks relevant to your brand
- Collectible cards, or a booklet
- Coupons for future orders

When we first started *Cashletes*, each order came delivered in a solid black box with our logo on top. It was awesome and unique, because it's rare that you come across a solid black box, and our customers loved it. Nowadays we've maintained a similar theme by packaging our hang-tagged products in glossy black poly bags with our logo on them, along with stickers in every order.

Keep in mind that presentation does a whole lot for your customers' purchase experience. It's fun and cool, and your shop should definitely utilize the individuality a unique package offers. Impressive t-shirt packaging can go a long way.

Don't Be Cheap

As you may have noticed, a common reminder throughout this book is to not be cheap. This is most important when it comes to producing your products. These are the highlights of your business, your source of income. You definitely don't want to end up with low-end products because you tried to spend as little money as possible.

It takes money to make money when producing t-shirts. But always keep in mind that although you may be dishing out your whole life savings, your invested money will multiply if you play it smart.

Print-On-Demand

Chances are you have some level of familiarity with "print-on-demand" fulfilment services such as **Cafe Press**, **Spreadshirt** and **Zazzle**. We depended on them in the early stages of our t-shirt selling ventures. Are they the best option when creating a clothing brand? Far from it. Sure, some people may have found success through their Cafe Press shops, but to be quite honest, selling your brand through these fulfilment companies will get you nowhere.

From a beginner's perspective, print-on-demand sounds perfect. You get to create as many t-shirt designs as you want, put them up for sale in your online shop, and the fulfilment company prints your t-shirts one by one as orders come in, without you having to do a thing. What sounds even greater is that you don't even have to pay them uprfront for all this. *They* pay *you* a percentage of each sale, so you can really only profit (as long as your sales revenue exceeds your low monthly membership fee). Perfect, right? More like false hope for aspiring t-shirt brand owners everywhere.

Consider this: Print-on-demand fulfilment services leave you at a severe disadvantage in many ways. For one, your t-shirts are limited in the ways they can look. Most of these services can only print your design at a maximum size of twelve by twelve inches, usually smaller. The print quality is also lacking, as these companies don't offer screen printing since the t-shirts are printed one at a time. Even worse, a customer will receive your t-shirt with a *Fruit Of The Loom* label on the inside and an advertisement for the company that printed the shirt. Awesome branding, huh?

If you're still thinking about giving print-on-demand a shot, this next fact will scare you. A t-shirt that you can get screen printed in bulk for about $8 will run up to $20 if produced through a print-on-demand fulfilment service. Add the tax and shipping, and you've got yourself a hefty $28 production cost for one mediocre quality t-shirt. Where's the room for profit?

Don't get me wrong, Cafe Press and the likes are good for what they're intended for. If you want a one-off just for yourself, get it through a print-on-demand service. You want personalized gifts, they've got you covered. Maybe you want to make random t-shirts with funny sentences on them to try and make a quick buck. Worth a shot, I guess. But as far as creating a top-notch t-shirt brand is concerned, don't waste your time. If you're serious about this, at least.

11

SET UP SHOP

These days, your website is your most important selling tool, especially as a new company without a budget that allows you to open your own brick-and-mortar store. When it comes to building a brand, if you don't have a website, you don't exist. There are several important aspects to running a profitable t-shirt selling website that we'll outline on the following pages.

Your Website

There are several steps to building the most effective online shop that not only sells products but also helps build a fan base. For starters, only offer products that you truly believe are of high quality. This is something you should handle during the product development process, because it will play a big part in online selling success. Some brand owners will complain that they have the perfect website, the perfect online shop, and have been marketing heavily, but still can't manage to make sales. One look at their shop and it's clear that the quality of their products is the real issue.

You should also know your customer very well. The easiest way to sell t-shirts is to have a good idea of the psychological factors that would turn a visitor into a customer. Knowing your customers well also gives you a head start. This is why it helps to be similar to your target customer yourself. That way, you'll already have an idea of the factors that influence you to buy something online and the kind of shopping experience you would want from an online store. Customer experience is one of the most important things to consider. Your shop should be memorable for positive reasons.

To run a t-shirt selling business, your website should be integrated with an e-commerce platform. This is essential. I've come across some t-shirt brand sites that lack an e-commerce system and instead have a message that reads "To buy one of our shirts, please contact us with the name of the shirt you want, your shirt size and your address, and send us money through PayPal." If that doesn't appear amateur to you, you've never shopped online before.

Look around at other brands' sites and you'll see what a clothing brand site should look like. A customer should be able to visit your site and make a purchase within a few clicks. Payments should be made by credit card or PayPal. Sadly, some potential customers are turned away when they discover that they can't purchase from your site using cash or writing a check. You'll be okay without those guys.

E-Commerce Necessities

The following elements are essential to the creation and functionality of your e-commerce website.

1) Easy Navigation

The goal of an e-commerce site is for the customer to leave with a purchase, and your navigation should reflect that goal. It should be extremely easy to go from the home page to the product selection page and ultimately to the cart/checkout page.

How To Do It: Have two separate navigation areas on your website. One as the main navigation, and the other as a secondary shop navigation to sort out product categories. The main navigation is best positioned horizontally across the top of the site. In the main navigation, it's important that you include: *Home, Shop, About, Cart, FAQ* and *Contact.* In the secondary shop navigation, include all of your product categories, including *New Products* and *On Sale.* Once your website is built, test the ease of use by asking a friend to attempt a purchase.

2) Great Product Images

Show your product in its best light. A great product image turns lookers into buyers and is one of the keys to the success of your online shop. Conversely, low-quality product images will ruin the chances of people buying from your shop.

How To Do It: Take high-quality photos of your t-shirts and enhance them using photo-editing software to achieve the best representation of the product. If you can't do it yourself, **YPU.org** has some good photographers. If you want the photos to include models, have your friends stand in as models, or hire models from **ModelMayhem.com**. Each product image should be at least 600px wide so it is large enough for potential buyers to see intricate details on a computer screen. Two to three alternate images of the product should also be included to give a good sense of what the product will look like in person.

3) Detailed Product Info

Each product should include detailed information, which can make or break a sale. Along with product images, this is one of the most important aspects of minimizing merchandise returns.

How To Do It: Describe everything from the obvious to the most detailed bits about the product. Be sure to include what the t-shirt is made of, the printing method or application used, and the colors of the t-shirt. Your product description should only be 1-3 sentences, so be sure to contain info that will give customers a good idea of what they are buying. You can also include a short, witty or interesting sentence or two about the product to extend your brand personality and further convince a potential customer to make a purchase.

4) Sizing Chart

Since your shop is online, visitors don't get to try your products on before buying them. Because of this, online shoppers have to buy products before getting to try them on, and a situation in which the customer orders a size that ends up being too loose or too tight will result in a return. To prevent this from happening, you need a sizing chart on your site that let's your visitors know the exact measurements of each shirt size you offer.

How To Do It: The best place to include your sizing chart is on the individual product page of every single item. There should be some type of link to a pop-up sizing chart, or a small image of the sizing chart that can be enlarged. Rather than measure each t-shirt size yourself, refer to the sizing chart already provided by the brand of t-shirt blanks you will be using. If your tees will be made from scratch, you'll already have provided the manufacturer with sizing details, so those will come in handy.

In addition to having a sizing chart, if your t-shirts don't fit true to size, make sure to specify that within your product description. We've had some **Cashletes** customers make returns or exchanges in the past due to certain products fitting a bit smaller than expected, so we made sure to state this in the description of those products.

5) Security

Even though we live in a day and age in which more and more people trust the Internet and provide their personal information to sites on a regular basis, people are still concerned about their safety online. You want assure your potential customers that your website is safe and trustworthy so that they are more likely to make a purchase.

How To Do It: The best way to make sure that your site is secure is to choose a shopping cart platform that processes payments securely. Almost every single shopping cart platform out there already does this, so you won't have to worry much about that. However, your visitors might not know that your shop is secure. To inform your visitors about your site's security, make sure to display security seals for the protection your shopping cart platform already has.

Our online shop is verified by **Paypal**, and Paypal keeps information secure with **VeriSign Identity Protection**. Therefore, we display the 'Paypal Verified' seal and the 'VeriSign Identity

Protection' seal on our shop to show that transactions are secure.

Make sure to also include information about your site's security in a sentence or two on your FAQ page. For example, the answer to a question such as "How secure is your shop?" would be: "This store uses PayPal for all transactions, and PayPal automatically encrypts your confidential information in transit from your computer to ours using the Secure Sockets Layer protocol (SSL) with an encryption key length of 128-bits (the highest level commercially available)."

As long as you choose an e-commerce platform that has the standard security features (**SSL protocool**, **Verisign**, and/or **McAffee Identity Protection**), your shop should already be secure. It's up to you to let your visitors know that, so they feel safe providing their credit card information on your site.

6) Payment Options

The payment options you should accept are credit/debit card and **Paypal**. If you want, you can include **Amazon Payments** or **Google Checkout** as an option, but only if it's already one of the default options for your e-commerce platform. Having other options, like paying by check or money order, just becomes a hassle and isn't worth dealing with.

The problem with having the customer send a check or money order is that checks can bounce, and there's a chance either method could get lost in transit. The majority of people who will be interested in buying from you will have either a debit/credit card or a Paypal account. Don't worry about the small percentage of sales you might be missing by not allowing check or money-order payments.

How To Do It: Create your online shop on an e-commerce platform that accepts credit/debit cards and Paypal. Highlight the payment options you accept on your shopping cart page, and be sure to display the logos of the four major credit card providers: VISA, MasterCard, American Express, and Discover.

7) Shipping and Returns Info

It's important to let potential customers know how much it'll cost to have their order shipped to them and how long it will take to receive the products they ordered. You may end up with an overload of abandoned shopping carts (meaning the customer added products to his/her cart but never completed the purchase) if you don't indicate shipping costs in advance. Details about how to process a return are also essential, especially if you hope to attract repeat customers.

How To Do It: You should factor in how much it'll cost *you* to ship products to your customers when deciding how much to charge for shipping. You should also check the website of your shipping carrier for the estimated delivery times of each shipping method that you'll be offering. It's best to offer more than one shipping option, such as Standard and Express.

You should include your shipping information either on the FAQ page or on a separate "Shipping and Returns" page. As for your product return and exchange requirements, decide on a time frame in which returns will be accepted and in what condition the merchandise must be to qualify. Indicate whether or not you will be paying the shipping costs for returns and exchanges as well. And of course, actually follow through with processing all returns and exchanges in the manner you state on your site.

8) FAQ

When you have questions about buying a product online, you take a look at the FAQ ("Frequently Asked Questions") page. When creating a FAQ page, you should aim to answer all of the questions you think your customers may have and add answers to questions that your customers have already asked you.

How To Do It: List all the common questions an online customer might have. It helps to look at the FAQ section of another brand's website and base your questions on theirs. Here are some questions to start off with:

- How do I checkout?
- Do you have sizing information?
- Which payment methods do you accept?
- How can I track my order?
- When will my order be shipped?
- Do you ship outside of the U.S.?
- How secure is this store?

These are some questions customers will consider asking either before they purchase or after they've purchased, and having an FAQ page provides immediate answers.

Choosing An E-Commerce Platform

There are several different e-commerce platforms out there to choose from, each with its advantages and disadvantages. The key is to keep in mind the particular features your business will require. Of course, all of these platforms allow you to achieve the ultimate goal: sales. But there's definitely more to these e-commerce platforms than simply allowing visitors to make a purchase. Here are our recommendations for platforms to consider using.

Big Cartel
Cost: $9.99 - $29.99/mo

Difficulty: Easy
Features: Intermediate

Big Cartel provides a shopping cart solution for independent artists and small shop owners that is simple to use. With Big Cartel, you're given full control of customizing the appearance of each page of your shop. You can even connect your Big Cartel shop with *Google Analytics E-Commerce Tracking* to track your sales statistics. There are a few advanced shopping cart features missing from this platform, but you might not even have an immediate need for these missing features. The most important thing is to get your feet wet and start selling, and Big Cartel is the quickest way to do that.

Big Commerce
Cost: $24.95 - $299.95/mo
Difficulty: Moderate
Features: Advanced

Big Commerce is a more advanced shopping cart solution that takes some time to get used to due to all the features and customization options. Some of those features include the ability to create customer loyalty programs, offer bulk discounts and create category-specific sales and discount codes. Big Commerce also integrates with accounting software like *MYOB* and *Peachtree*. The great thing about this is that the accounting for your online sales will be almost completely automated, and if you're not really a numbers person, this will save you some headaches.

Core Commerce
Cost: $19.99 - $219.99/mo
Difficulty: Moderate
Features: Advanced

Like Big Commerce, Core Commerce is also a more advanced shopping cart platform. Actually, Core Commerce's features are very similar to those of Big Commerce: You have great control over up-selling features, you can run category-specific sales, and the back-end administration interface for both platforms is very similar. Core Commerce also offers integration with accounting software, but unlike Big Commerce, you can also integrate with **Quickbooks** accounting software.

Battle Of The Shopping Carts

We don't want to go too deep into explaining every single feature of each shopping cart platform, since the platform you choose out of these three won't have much of an impact on the development of your brand. To summarize, if you have a small budget and you want to start selling your products as soon as possible, you should go with Big Cartel. If you're selling a large collection of products with many different variants and you don't mind minor complications in a shopping cart platform if it means advanced features, Core Commerce or Big Commerce should do it for you.

Start A Blog

Blogging has become one of the biggest Internet trends of the new millennium. Everybody and their momma has a blog: from businesses looking to maximize their online presence, to individuals trying to make a name for themselves, and even regular people who simply want to keep a journal online. Nearly every clothing brand website I come across these days has a blog, so it's becoming a standard. The top three blog providers are *Wordpress.org*, *Blogger.com*, and *Tumblr.com*.

If you're someone who just can't keep up with daily blog posting, consider including a section on your site similar to a blog that you can host on a blogging platform (a "News" section, for instance). We've tried the daily posts thing once before and realized it was hard to keep up with since we were doing so many other things at the same time (going to school, developing other businesses, freelance work, etc.), so we took a different approach. The **Cashletes** site has a "Features" section instead. There, we post new updates as frequently as we can, but not as frequently as the typical blog.

Here are some reasons you should have a blog, or something similar, on your website.

To Stay Connected

One of the best ways to increase sales is by connecting with your customers. Writing a blog can keep you connected with the people who like your clothing and want to know more about your brand or even about you as a person. When you read a t-shirt brand's blog, it almost feels as if you know the writer personally. You can upload your latest photos, videos or stories for your customers to keep up with the brand's development.

To Have Fun

If you're an avid reader of blogs, you can tell that bloggers have lots of fun writing them. It's your chance to just have fun and ease the stress of running a business. If you come off as cool, humorous and interesting, you may attract customers simply because they enjoyed the personality you convey in your blog posts.

Attract Return Visits

If you're like most clothing brands, your shop won't update every day (or every week, for that matter), since you won't be releasing new products that often. That leaves customers with no reason to come back every few days. Having a blog that is updated regularly will have fans visiting your site all the time to see if there's anything new. Your biggest fans will anticipate your next blog post just as they anticipate your next t-shirt release. With all these return visits, a browser can become a customer, and a customer can become a repeat customer.

A Good Site Design

We've all seen a bad site design before. You know, a site you can barely stand to look at for more than five seconds before your eyes start tearing up, and they aren't tears of joy. If you've already got a website for your brand, your site design probably sucks and you don't even realize it. When a site has a bad design, it may be a matter of taste, but more likely it's a matter of poor quality execution. If you've got bad taste, we can't help you there, but as far as execution goes, here are some pointers to what a good site looks like.

1) Conveys the Visual Brand Identity

Most importantly, a good site design matches the rest of the visual aspects of your brand identity. You'll notice that brands with awesome site designs always have a certain kick of flavor in their design that really fits their entire brand image.

2) A Font that's Easy to Read

The main font you use in your shop and on your blog should be clearly legible. Of the HTML fonts available to you (in web design, the main font is limited to a select few HTML-compatible fonts), our font of choice is Helvetica. Also, keep the font either black, white or gray, unless you're specifically highlighting some important piece of text. Colored text can be uncomfortable to read sometimes.

3) Limited Color Scheme

Try to keep the colors in your site design down to a maximum of three, unless your brand is about rainbows or something. These colors should match the colors of your visual brand identity.

4) Same Size Product Images

All of the product images in your shop should be the same exact dimensions and orientation. It sounds obvious, but you wouldn't believe the number of new shops we've seen with images of all sorts of shapes and sizes (making the shop look choppy and unorganized), so this had to be mentioned.

5) No Blurry Images

Make sure every image is crisp and clear—everything from the logo in the header to the product photos. Seriously, not even the slightest bit of blurriness can pass. Nothing should look unintentionally pixelated either. Sharp images make all the difference.

Designing And Creating Your Site

Now that we've told you all that goes into a good online shop, it would make sense to inform you on how to actually get your site made. Sorry, we won't give you a whole tutorial on how to create your website step-by-step, but we will tell you what is required.

First off, creating your website on your own is only recommended if you happen to be a web designer or a digital artist interested in web design. There's a huge learning curve for anybody who isn't familiar with graphic design, so if you aren't a graphic designer, you should hire a professional to create your website for you. Some good web design companies are **The Black**

Axe, **DoubleDragon Studios** and **The Neon Hive**. Expect to pay anywhere from $500 to $3,000 for a web design.

If your budget is pretty small and you're not sure if you can shell out $500 to $3,000 on a fully customized website design, then your best bet would be to use a pre-made website template. Certain e-commerce platforms already offer free templates to choose from. You can also do an online search for templates compatible with the e-commerce and blog platform that you're using.

With a website template, you should be able to upload your logo and graphics and do some color and font changes, allowing you to create the look that you're going for. Your site design won't necessarily be exactly what you had in mind, but you'll still have a great-looking site for a fraction of the cost of hiring a web designer.

If you think you are capable of designing and creating a site on your own, you'll need a digital art program like **Photoshop** or **Illustrator** to create the design. What you create in these programs will be a mock-up of what the actual site will look like (similar to the mock-ups you'd create for your t-shirt designs), so every element of the design should be designed in the exact dimensions you want them to appear online. Take a screen capture of your Internet browser to have a set of dimensions to work from.

The mock-up is the easy part that any artist could manage to create. But after creating the mock-up, things get pretty complex, so we can't dive into all those technicalities within the pages of this book. There are entire books written on web design (rather lengthy ones, too), so we'll keep this short and just suggest you Google "web design tutorials" and "HTML tutorials" for all that. If you're able to create a well-designed mock-up but don't know how to actually code websites, luckily you can hire someone to handle the coding aspect of your site. But if web design is not your thing, we'd strongly suggest hiring a web designer to get the job done in a professional manner, or purchase a website template.

12

MARKETING YOUR BRAND

To build a high demand for your brand, you must market like there's no tomorrow. A good marketing plan will take your brand from "Never heard of that before" to "I need that!" The marketing you do for your brand isn't just limited to buying ads. There are several aspects of marketing, free and paid, online and offline, on your site and external to your site, that must be considered when creating an ultimate marketing plan.

Promoting Your Website

The phrase "If you build it, they will come" does not apply in the world wide web. Once you've created an outstanding website, you'll have to work on attracting customers by promoting it. The following are the best ways to do so.

Online Ad Campaign

One of the most efficient ways to promote a website is with an online advertising campaign. As opposed to offline advertising, online advertising makes it easier for a potential customer to go from seeing your ad to purchasing your product, since your website is only one click away.

The key to a successful online ad campaign is showing your ad on a targeted site with a good amount of traffic. A targeted site is one that your intended customer visits regularly. A "good" amount of traffic for a website is at least 800 visitors per day. Usually, the more visits a site gets per day, the higher the advertising rate, so be sure to compare traffic and ad rates for different sites before choosing which to run your campaign on.

Your best bet is to set a moderate advertising budget and shop around for advertising opportunities. A good starting budget would be $100-250. Anything less and you are unlikely to see any results.

Google AdWords

The first weapon in your advertising arsenal should be *Google AdWords*. As a new brand, Google AdWords' CPC ("cost-per-click") plan is the best method for advertising your brand online. In other words, you only pay when someone clicks on your ad. Hypothetically, if you got absolutely no clicks over the course of your campaign, you'd be advertising for free. This minimizes the risk of wasting your advertising dollars. You get to broadcast your ads on a multitude of websites, and you only pay if someone clicks on your ad.

We don't recommend **CPM ads** early on. With a CPM campaign, you pay for impressions rather than clicks. This means if you get absolutely no clicks throughout your campaign, you will still end up paying for the ad. The only way to beat the risk of CPM ads is to have a high click-through rate, which is possible once you've gotten the hang of creating ads that yield such results. It's unlikely that your ad would have a high click-through rate in the beginning, since you haven't mastered advertising optimization yet.

Press Coverage

Press coverage is the best form of free advertising you can get to promote your brand. A reputable publication announcing your news to it's readers is a cosign that gives your new brand much-needed credibility. But in order to get to the point where your brand is buzzed about all over the Internet, you'll have to have something worth talking about.

We've been lucky enough to play both sides of the press coverage game, running T-Shirt Magazine and Cashletes. Our plan for getting press coverage for the release of Cashletes was simple. Here's what it all came down to:

1) Making sure we were noteworthy in the first place.
This is something that should be done way before you contact the press, but many people seem to skip this step. You can't expect editors and bloggers to want to write about you if your products aren't high quality. The impression your website gives off plays a big part.

2) Making a list of sites that might be interested in what we were offering.
How did we know which sites would be interested in featuring our brand? We based it on the other brands they had previously

featured. When you identify your competitors and monitor their exposure, making this list becomes easy. You can easily search for a competitor on Google and see all the sites that mention them. Visit those sites and email them press releases (see steps 3 and 4).

3) Writing a straight-to-the-point message with important details.

We made it clear to the editors why we were contacting them, what we had to offer, and why their readers would care about us. It was no longer than two to three sentences.

4) Coming up with a catchy subject title.

When editors and bloggers receive your email, the first thing they'll see is the subject title, and it could be your one shot at getting them to open up your message. Make it a headline rather than just a generic "New Tees By [Insert Brand Name Here]." We included a very brief summary of our brand's theme in our subject line.

As editors of T-Shirt Magazine, we receive emails every day from brands requesting to be featured on our site, and it has become clear which brands have a better shot. We recently added a page of submission tips, outlining how to increase your chances of a write-up or interview.

For a better chance at coverage, follow these tips:

1) Include important details.

Highlight what readers should know about your products and where to buy them. This makes it easy for the customer to make a purchase, which makes selling easier for you.

2) Contact us about news.

Let us know about a specific collection release or new t-shirt, for example, rather than sending us information about your entire brand in general. This gives the editor a specific thing to post about, which is easier than a full-on brand profile.

3) Have a nice-looking website.
This includes awesome product shots, too. It makes the editors feel more comfortable recommending your products.

4) Offer something to our readers.
A coupon code or a t-shirt giveaway would be a great add-on that is worth mentioning. Offering the editors something could also work if they happen to like your product.

5) Keep it short.
Sometimes a long email with extensive details and background info may be put off for later reading and is subsequently lost in the jumble, so a shorter, more concise message is better.

Newsletter Promo

Have a mailing list sign-up box on your website, even before you have products for sale. We did just that when we started Cashletes, and we were able to gather e-mails of potential customers. With a mailing list, you have a group of people who volunteered to get all the latest news from your brand, so you know they're already interested in buying.

Send a newsletter at least once a month, highlighting the most important updates, product releases, coupon codes and sales. People love sales and discounts. However, make sure that these sales and discount promotions still allow room for you to actually profit. There's little use in holding a 70%-off sale if you're going to end up with no profit.

For a great newsletter platform, we'd recommend using either **Constant Contact** or **Mail Chimp**.

Search Engine Optimization

Also known as *SEO*, search engine optimization refers to strategic programming of your website so it appears on the first page of Google's search engine results. There's a lot that goes into it, including some HTML code that won't translate too well within the pages of this book.

Most importantly, the *meta title* of your website should always include descriptive terms in addition to your brand name. The meta title is basically the text that shows at the very top of a browser when on a website. It's also the title of the page when it appears in search engine results. It should reflect the content of your website so people looking for relevant content would be inclined to click on the link to get to your website.

Here's an example using a fictional ballet-themed brand, Glissade. Having the phrase "Glissade – Stylish Ballet T-Shirts and Ballerina Clothing" is better than just having "Glissade" as the meta title. The reason is that the first title includes terms that a potential customer might search for on Google, which would lead them to Glissade.com. If the people at Glissade only include their brand name in the meta title, a potential customer would be highly unlikely to find the site on Google unless he or she specifically searched for the keyword "Glissade."

Targeted content is also a very important on-site SEO tactic. The search engine decides if Glissade.com is the right site for the potential customer by browsing through all the text written on the site. If the text includes a lot of information on ballet t-shirts and other ballet related things, Google shows the site in its search results for relevant search terms. At the same time, you want to be careful not to include your main keyword too many times within the description, because Google will sense this as "black hat SEO" (using unethical techniques to improve your search ranking).

If the content of your site is comprised of a wide array of random stuff, like blog posts about what you ate for lunch that day, or your new puppy, you can confuse the search engine into thinking your site isn't relevant to the potential customer's search. In other words, keep all the content on your site relevant to the search terms you're aiming for so that potential customers are led to your site.

This is one of the reasons why it's important to keep your blog posts (and any other content on your site) relevant to the theme of your brand. When your content is targeted, people may come to your site via a search engine by accident. A ballet fan might be searching for the best ballet schools in the nation, and a post on the Glissade blog that lists such schools comes up as a search result on Google. She clicks the link and finds what she was looking for, but she also discovers a new t-shirt brand she likes. Just like that, a new potential customer becomes aware of the brand.

There is also a such thing as off-site SEO. One of the most important off-site SEO tactics is getting other reputable sites to link to yours. This is a secondary benefit of press coverage. You can even take it a step further by requesting that the website editor uses your keywords or terms as the link text. For example, you can request that the text "Stylish Ballet T-Shirts" appears in a link to Glissade.com. By doing this, the site linking to yours is telling Google that your site does in fact serve as a targeted destination for ballet t-shirts (or whatever your keywords are).

Matt McManus On Creating A Marketing Strategy

Gaining a brand following is one of the most important things to focus on while building a brand. Increasing the number of brand followers increases your sales and ultimately opens up the door to expand product lines and create the brand of your dreams. However, for a brand built from the ground up, building a dedicated following is one of the most difficult tasks to accomplish.

It doesn't happen overnight, it doesn't happen easily, and it *certainly* doesn't happen without dedication and commitment. But with a little bit of strategy and the proper approach, marketing campaigns and promotional tactics can result in your brand reaching incredible heights.

For an emerging brand, the fundamental goal of marketing campaigns and promotional schemes is to increase brand awareness. You want people who have never heard of your brand to visit your site and purchase your products. Beyond that, you want to build a *following.* Increased sales are good, but increased followers are *great.* If you can effectively build a consumer base that supports your brand for the long run rather than one-time buyers purchasing a single shirt, your promotional strategies are working. The question is, how can you effectively create campaigns that do more than drive added traffic to your website?

Marketing campaigns, and brand image as a whole, must attempt to connect with consumers on a personal level. If there is a face that consumers can easily match with the clothing that they are buying, they will be far more likely to identify with and support the brand. Successful streetwear brands like The Hundreds, Benny Gold, and Johnny Cupcakes give fans more than a brand. They give them a lifestyle that they can identify with, and instead of supporting a business, they are supporting a person.

Several steps can be taken to effectively promote your brand online. First, contacting as many blogs, online magazines and streetwear news sites with your current product releases is vital. To give yourself the best "chance" of receiving exposure on these sites, you must make sure that the product you are presenting to them is clean, professional and unique. Before sending an email or placing a phone call, take a look at the content that publication usually features and ask yourself if what you are showing them would fit in nicely with their current content. If you *truly* believe that your content matches, then you can be confident in your communication with the owners of these various outlets.

Traditional Internet advertising campaigns will do amazing things for your brand. They will show buyers, competitors and consumers that your brand is a heavy-hitter in the industry. Unfortunately, for many brands starting out small, this is often financially difficult to accomplish. Many of the sites that you would like to approach with an advertising campaign will give you a $2,000 minimum. As a result, promotion online in an economically feasible manner can be accomplished by pushing for brand features and approaching smaller start-up blogs and online magazines for your advertising campaigns.

Additional non-traditional tactics can be used to promote your brand online by including key features on your website. Again, the intended effect of these features is to connect with consumers on a personal level. Offering wallpapers for download and enabling fans to join a street team will make them feel as if they have a hand in the brand. You can also send personal notes with each shipped package, adding that extra personal touch that tells them you're not just an average t-shirt brand!

To *really* make your push for online visibility effective, cross-promotion on several sites is optimal. Then, as your target consumers maneuver from site to site, they will see your brand every step of the way. Often, when consumers see something once, they may disregard the importance or relevance of it altogether. However, if you can make sure that your brand is showcased on at least two or more of the sites that your potential fans visit, your push will prove to be very effective. If consumers don't give your brand attention after seeing it once, they sure will after seeing it four times!

To conclude, several strategies can be developed to promote your brand online in a cost-effective, concise manner. With each product release, it is crucial that every single relevant blog and online magazine is contacted with photographs and any additional promotional materials. To make sure the response from these outlets is what you expect, present a product that you feel matches the content that they currently showcase.

Next, advertise where it is economically feasible to do so, and make sure that these advertising campaigns stay true to the brand image that you have created. If you have allocated a substantial number of costs to advertising online, focus these campaigns on sites that you feel most closely match your brand. Create campaigns that consumers can identify with, and include various elements on your website that make the customer feel as if they are part of the brand.

By implementing these tactics, soon your brand will go from being just a few shirts known only to your close family, to an internationally distributed powerhouse. It won't happen overnight, and it will not happen without a professional, unique product appeal. But indeed, it *can* happen, and it *will* happen if you believe in yourself and in your brand.

Marc McMannus is the founder of CheckYourSix
(www.CheckYourSix.com)

Pricing Your T-Shirts

One of the major aspects of marketing that affects your chances of sales, and a good profit, is the pricing of your products. It can be tricky deciding on the proper pricing, but once you've got your branding and production planned out, it'll be easier to make this decision. Your pricing, among other things, will affect your profit.

There are a few common price ranges for t-shirts:

$10 - $15 range
These shirts are usually found among new brands that plan on going with the "cheap shirts" approach or among brands that have been around for a while and can afford huge bulk orders that allow them to sell their t-shirts for low costs while still making a good profit.

$16 - $24 range
This is the unofficial average price range for the majority of t-shirt brands. Most brands you come across will have their tees at this price range whether they're new or have been around for a while. It offers a great profit margin if you can afford huge orders, and a good-enough margin if you place small wholesale orders.

$25 - $30 range
These tees usually come off as being higher quality than the average tees and often involve designs that feature various print locations, multiple print techniques or all-over prints. Many streetwear labels—rookies and vets alike—go with this range.

$31 - $60 range

Upscale labels often pull off this price range. These tees are often associated with high quality, luxury, affluence and sophistication and also have more complex production processes. Or the brand is just so popular the name sells itself. The labels are also often endorsed by and marketed towards celebs or fashion industry vets, which allows the retail price to be so high.

When choosing a price range for your brand, keep in mind these key characteristics within each range. Determine which range best defines your brand or which prices you'd like your shirts to be sold for. Be realistic, too. Some newbies make the mistake of trying to create expensive upscale labels without offering high-quality t-shirts or having any celebrity backing.

A good thing to do is to check the pricing of competitors. Do yours match up? Are they lower or higher? Try to keep your pricing within the same range as other brands in your niche. You might be thinking, "I'll sell my tees cheaper than my competition so that people prefer mine!" This isn't always the case. Only offer cheaper prices if you can still promise equal or better quality. Otherwise, you'll just come off as a knock-off wannabe brand. The "CHEAP, CHEAP, CHEAP!" approach isn't necessarily the best route to take.

The price points mentioned above are specifically for straight-to-customer sales. When you sell your products in bulk to retail shops, also known as wholesale, pricing is different.

Typically, retailers will take your product and sell it for two times as much as they bought it for. If your retail price is $20, your wholesale price should be $10. This is what the price ranges above would look like as wholesale prices:

$10 - $15 retail = $5 - $7.50 wholesale

$16 - $24 retail = $8 - $12 wholesale

$25 - $30 retail = $12.50 - $15 wholesale

$31 - $60 retail = $15.50 - $30 wholesale

Are you ready to offer your t-shirts for these wholesale prices? Will you still be able to profit? Here's an equation you should try to use to figure out the minimum price you can sell your tees for:

Production cost x 2 = Wholesale price
Wholesale price x 2 = Retail price

Keep these things in mind when deciding on the pricing for your t-shirts. As with many business journeys, you may find that not all this pricing stuff is the same everywhere or that your particular situation requires you to price differently. If so, adjust as necessary.

Social Networking

Back in the days of our first t-shirt brand, most of our online customers came through **Myspace**, which at that time was at its prime. Nowadays, we use **Facebook** and **Twitter** to promote Cashletes. Social networking is a powerful tool for promoting your brand, and it's no surprise that many of the top brands today utilize social networking to expand their online presence and resonate with the tech-savvy youth market.

The best approach to marketing through social networking is to create a profile on at least two of the top social networking sites. Currently, Facebook and Twitter are the two, so we have both a Facebook page and a Twitter profile for Cashletes and T-Shirt Magazine.

For the best results, treat your profile like your website. First off, design it with a similar look to keep up with your brand image. Facebook has an HTML application called *FBML* which allows you to create a landing tab on your Facebook page that you can design to look like your website (by using HTML and CSS). I barely see any upcoming brands utilize this feature, but all the big companies use it, so doing so yourself would help your brand make a great first impression.

Always keep content fresh and notify people of all the latest news and sales. The easiest way to do this is by linking your website and newsletter to each of your social networking profiles so that updates are automatic. That way, you minimize the maintenance of your social networking profiles.

There's a service called **TwitterFeed** that tweets the title of your blog posts automatically, and Facebook has an option to import your blog posts in their entirety to your page as *Notes*. You can also post your newsletter content to your social network pages. **Constant Contact** has an option to feed links to your newsletter announcements through Twitter. Other newsletter platforms may also have similar features. Once you have your social networking automated, there is minimal work required on your part to keep your profiles updated.

Besides having a fresh profile, you also need people to "Like" your page on Facebook and "follow" you on Twitter. The first step towards gaining fans and followers is to have links to your brand's Facebook and Twitter pages. Almost every clothing brand website out there has a little Facebook and Twitter icon linking to their social network accounts. People who visit your site are likely to make their way to your Facebook and Twitter profiles if you provide the links.

A good way to start receiving "Likes" on your Facebook page is to recommend the page to your current Facebook friends. By recommending your page to all of your Facebook friends, those that are at least mildly interested will "Like" your page. Your current Facebook friends may not actually buy anything from you, but *their* friends might "Like" your page after seeing that your friend liked the page, and this momentum will continue to build. So it may very well end up being a "friend of a friend of a friend" who ends up buying your t-shirts.

This might sound like a long process, but as soon as a couple people start "Liking" your page, the number of "Likes" you receive begins to increase very quickly, and before you know it, you'll have hundreds of people getting notified about your brand's updates.

A way to gain followers on Twitter is by following other people who might be interested in your brand. When you follow someone, they're likely return the favor and follow you. When following other people, make sure to only follow people who might actually be interested in your brand. This can include the general public, celebrities, and the press. If your brand is targeted toward college guys who like to party, following people like Bill Clinton, *Seventeen Magazine*, or a random 35-year-old lady wouldn't make any sense and would be a waste of time. Instead, follow people who fit your target customer description and websites and celebrities who appeal to your target customers.

When people "Like" or "follow" you, they will be notified every time you post something on Facebook or Twitter. This makes social network marketing a great way to reach out to those who are already pre-sold on your brand. Similar to newsletter marketing, sending notifications to people who have expressed interest in your brand could give them the nudge they need that could ultimately turn a "will buy some day" mentality into a "must buy now."

Up-Selling Tactics

This is basic on-site marketing. If your shopping cart platform allows for it, offer deals that encourage customers to purchase more than one item at once. This increases the checkout amount per order, consequently leading to more revenue. Some common up-selling examples are "buy one, get one 50% off" and "buy any two, get a coupon for your next order" promotions. Since the customer will be saving money by making a purchase of more than one product, whether the savings are immediate or can be applied later, the customer will include additional products in his purchase.

The other way to up-sell is by offering other types of products that your customers might be interested in, such as sticker packs, accessories and other apparel. A good way to set up this kind of up-sell is by having the up-sell product available for purchase right from the cart page. For example, let's say the customer adds a t-shirt to their cart. When the customer gets to the cart page, he'll see the t-shirt he chose in the cart ready to purchase and, below the cart area on that page, a link to your up-sell product. On our web shop, we put these up-sell products in a section headlined "And Why Not."

Since the customer is already in buying mode, they probably won't mind adding a low-price item such as stickers. Adding a few extra dollars to a customer order here and there will begin to add up, leading to higher revenue. This tactic is very similar to what supermarkets do by putting things like candy, soda bottles and magazines right at the checkout aisles to tempt you to add these items to your purchase.

As a preliminary up-sell tactic (before the customer even gets to the cart page), on the individual product page for each product you can include links to two or three related products at the bottom of the page. Label them as "Similar Products" or "You May Also Like…" These up-sell products can be equal in value to the product on the individual product page the customer is viewing and serve as a way to suggest another product the customer might like. It's not as tempting as the checkout page up-sell method, but the customer may still consider purchasing the additional product.

Another up-sell method is discounted or free shipping for orders above a certain dollar amount. Currently on our clothing brand site, we offer free shipping on all orders over $100. This method tends to work really well with our international customers since international shipping rates for orders under $100 are relatively high. Providing free shipping for orders above a certain dollar amount becomes a win-win situation: the customer doesn't have to worry about paying shipping costs, and you end up with greater revenue since the customer is ordering more products.

In addition, since shipping multiple products together as one package equates to a lower shipping cost *per product* than shipping one item alone, you end up saving more money when you pay for shipping. Having a free shipping incentive also prevents the chance of a customer deciding to wait to buy an additional product later, only to end up not purchasing that additional product at all. Repeat customers are great, but why not get a customer who will purchase multiple products within their first order *and* make a repeat purchase later?

Trade Shows And Conventions

Besides promoting your brand online, it is important to build your face-to-face presence as well. Exhibiting at trade shows and conventions is a great way to market your brand and sell your products directly to your customer base and potential retailers in a live-action arena. It usually costs at least a couple hundred dollars to exhibit at a show that would give you a decent amount of exposure, so I'd recommend holding off on exhibiting until you've begun generating a decent cash flow.

Just to give you a general idea, a booth at one of the major trade shows in the nation, ***Magic***, runs around $2,500 minimum, and that's not even counting your actual display setup. Furthermore, in some cases you must pay for your booth at least six months in advance. Even so, exhibiting at Magic or another major trade show should definitely be in your plans, as it will put your brand amongst some of the other top brands in the world and give retailers an opportunity to do business with you.

David Murray's Tips on Exhibiting at Shows

From small street festivals to large events that can bring in tens of thousands of potential fans, selling tees at live events is not only a great source of potential income but also a great way to introduce yourself and your brand to people firsthand. With research, preparation and hard work on the day of the show, you can find the right event for you and make a big splash. You can also receive important feedback about aspects your audience responds to.

Research

Finding the right show is important. You want to find something appropriate for your level that will also be attended by your target audience.

If you're just starting out and only have a few designs, maybe it's not time to drop a couple grand for a booth at *Bamboozle* or *Comic-Con*. Even if we assume that you have great products and are completely awesome, you need to start off with smaller shows to get some experience under your belt.

Think of it as leveling up. Starting with small shows will also help you get a sense of how much inventory to bring to future shows and will allow you to build up your in-person salesman skills, so by the time you do have that big tent at *Vans Warped Tour* or *New York Comic Con* or whatever, you'll be a pro.

This next part is common sense, so I'll keep it short: No matter how good your product is, if you try to sell it to the wrong audience, it's probably not going to do well. Think about your target audience and what venues and events they might attend. Look at brands you like that are similar to yours, and see what kind of shows they frequent.

Preparation

When you're at the show, you basically need to put the same consideration you put into your website into your booth or table. Although it varies from event to event, you will almost never be the main attraction.

It will be just like the Internet: thousands of people may pass by, but they will have other things on their mind ("Where's the next band playing?" "Where can I buy some beer?" "Where's the pornography?"), and you may only have a second to catch their attention and interest them enough to come over and actually look at all of your hard work. Just as a well-made website will get people to stop surfing and start spending, an eye catching, professional-looking booth can get people talking and wallets opening.

How you decorate your booth is up to you and your brand, but keeping certain fundamentals in mind will make things easier for you. Design it so anyone who looks at your booth knows the name of your brand and what you're selling. Have a big banner with your name and website address on it, and have your products prominently displayed so no one will have any question as to who you are and what you're selling.

Make sure that anyone walking into your booth can see all of your products just by glancing around. Though methods and practices vary, having all of your products displayed (ideally hanging up at eye level) will increase the chances that people walking by your booth will see something they like and stop to look. Once I'm done setting up my booth at a show, I always walk by from every possible point of approach to make sure I've got some of my proven favorites and bestsellers on display from every angle and make sure the setup looks good.

Be different. I can't tell you how to be different, but I always try to do something interesting with my booth display. Anything to get a second look from people. I've created Post-It mosaics that took me 12 hours just to stick to the inside of my booth (and many hours before that of planning). I've even made huge standees for people to take pictures with. Just try to think of something that would get you excited and get you talking, and then go for it.

People don't want to watch you look for stuff. If someone asks if you have a certain product in their size, you should be so well-organized that a quick glance at your shelving or boxes of shirts should answer their question immediately. Having to dig through unorganized boxes makes you look sloppy, wastes everyone's time, and lessens the chance of sealing the deal.

Use fanny packs, not cash boxes. As someone who once had a cashbox with nearly $4,000 in it stolen (long story that ended with me cussing really loudly), it's much better to have your money on you at all times rather than sitting in some box. Maybe you don't want to wear a fanny pack, in which case, just be careful. Seriously.

Have a friend who will work with you! This is the best, and it helps to lighten the load. The one time I hired someone I didn't know at all, it was super awkward, but I have so many great memories of working with people I love. It will put you in a good mood, which will make you more approachable.

The Day(s) of the Show

If you're well prepared, then the actual show should be a piece of cake, right? Here are some important things to remember.

Work. You're there to work. It's fun, yes, and you get to meet new people and make friends, but you've got to work hard and sell things, too! Just getting to sell something is a privilege. If you have a friend working with you, don't goof off with them too much—fun work is still work.

Don't take it too personally. You don't actually witness this on the Internet, but plenty of people see your stuff every day, decide they don't like it, and move on. Get ready to have it happen in person! Don't worry, though, because seeing those people that flip out and love your work and call their friends over will make it more than worth it.

Be nice, and give people time. People remember this kind of stuff. Also, don't flash too much cash when you open your fanny pack or cash box. Try to regularly drop cash in a safe location (say, locked inside your car). I've learned this the hard way.

After the Show

Hopefully, the show was a smashing success. You met lots of new fans, maybe even got a celebrity or two in your gear, and are coming home with lighter boxes and a fat fanny pack. But, sometimes shows don't go so well – the weather is bad, or the crowds just aren't there, or maybe it just wasn't a good match for you.

Keep your chin up and keep going! Either way, think about how people responded to certain things; it's a gift to be able to see customers' reactions in person, good or bad. Every show is a learning experience, so figure out what you can do better, and use this knowledge to make the next one a hit.

**David Murray is the creator of Seibei
(www.Seibei.com)**

Creating a Lookbook

When creating a clothing line, one of the most important things is presentation. You can have the best t-shirts in the world, but if they're not presented the right way, they might not create the impact you're looking for. A lookbook is a great way to present your clothing.

A lookbook is a seasonally released set of photographs that represents your brand image. Unlike a catalog, photos in a lookbook usually depict the clothing models reenacting real-life situations or are posed in an artistic manner rather than simply standing in front of the camera (although some brands do take this approach). Many of the top brands in the fashion industry create lookbooks to complement each new collection they release.

Creating a lookbook for your brand is your opportunity to demonstrate the image you're trying to pull off and highlight the audience you're targeting through a visual language. Your lookbook can be a printed book or a digital collection of images on your brand's website.

The following are some tips on creating a lookbook for your clothing line:

1) Check Out Some Other Lookbooks First

It'll help to get an idea of what the finished product should look like. Also, if you see that other brands in your niche do not have lookbooks, your brand probably shouldn't have one either.

2) Hire a Professional Photographer

Or get your hands on a high-quality camera. You're going to need one if you want impressive photos. Nothing is worse than an upcoming brand with a crappy photo shoot.

3) Decide On Some Cool Locations

Maybe you want that grunge look with some brick and concrete or a modern look with a minimalistic environment and solid colors. Maybe you just want some shots of a few friends hanging out at your favorite fast-food place. Pick something that fits the brand.

4) Consider Using Props

Have the models interact with furniture, automobiles, food, electronics, animals, instruments, toys—whatever you want. It will make the photo a little more interesting.

5) Gather a Bunch of Your Friends

Most of them should fit the image of your label since they're *your* friends and *you* fit the image of your label. Get them to wear your t-shirts and pose. Hiring models isn't as fun.

6) Be the Director

Have your friends pose in the locations you pick with the props you choose. Have fun with it. It's up to you to make sure everything looks good.

7) Take the Same Picture More Than Once

It's good to have many options to choose from for each shot. This goes for shooting any kind of photo for your brand, whether it's for a lookbook or a product shot on the website.

8) Pick the Best Photos

Go through all the shots you've taken and narrow the set down to the best ones. Choose one to two shots for each t-shirt. Make sure you have at least six photos in the end, composed of group shots and individual shots.

9) Edit Your Final Set of Photos

Touch them up a little in **Photoshop**, make any necessary size adjustments, and crop them where necessary. You can even take it as far as adding illustration or other funky design elements to the photos.

10) Add the Lookbook to Your Website

Having a lookbook slideshow on your home page or elsewhere on your website always looks awesome.

Now you've got all the images you need to present and market your clothing brand. Although a lookbook is not 100% necessary, it could help potential customers get a better understanding of the vision behind your brand, which in turn can generate new fans. In addition, it's a great marketing tool, as you can announce the release of your lookbook to blog writers and use the photos as part of your ad campaign.

Product Placement

An effective strategy used by many indie clothing brands is getting their t-shirts on the bodies of famous or semi-famous personalities. This is the strategy of product placement on musicians, athletes, actors, or anybody else who fits the brand's image. Celebrity endorsements can make your brand "cool" overnight, especially when your target market really looks up to and idolizes the celebrities who endorse your products.

Getting famous people to wear your t-shirts can sometimes be a matter of knowing the right people. Having connections to celebrities may be the easiest way to get endorsements, so ask around. Becoming a popular clothing brand through your other hard work methods is another easy way to get an endorsement; a celebrity may just happen to buy one of your t-shirts on their own.

Celebrity stylists are also always on the lookout for the next hot clothing brand to style their clients in, and it could be yours. We've been contacted on a few occasions to supply clothing for a photoshoot or video shoot that a music artist was involved in. We didn't employ any special strategy or extra planning to get these requests; we simply kept up our good work, and as a result, people love our stuff enough to want to endorse our brand. I think that's the best method of getting celebrity endorsements. Don't rush it, and just keep building on your brand until you begin to catch the eye of celebrities and their associates.

Some brands have to work harder for product placement on celebrities. In some cases, you might have to go the extra mile and reach out to celebrity stylists (or perhaps the celebrities themselves) to pitch your t-shirt brand. Your best bet would be to find out who's styling who, and how you can get in contact with that person. Narrow your search down to a specific person to make it easier. Search "Taylor Swift's stylist," for example. Nowadays, you can even get in direct contact with celebrities through social networks like **Twitter**, so you might even be able to score an endorsement deal that way.

Overall, I truly believe the "get big until you get noticed" approach is the best way to get endorsed by celebrities. This way, they're coming to you rather than *you* putting all your effort into getting *their* attention. You're better off spending your time building your brand in other ways.

Also, even though a celebrity endorsement has the potential to skyrocket your brand image, it may not exactly skyrocket your sales. Just something to consider when developing your marketing plan. In the end, a celebrity endorsement at one point or another is definitely a good look.

13

GETTING INTO STORES

If you're serious about making it big in the industry, selling in stores should be a major part of your business plan. Many aspiring clothing brand owners see this as the ultimate achievement and their big ticket to super-stardom. It really is a satisfying goal to reach, and it can be done easily with the right tactics.

A Whole New Ball Game

Selling in stores is a completely different challenge than selling online. Getting the privilege to sell in stores in the first place is a journey of its own, involving cold-calling, face-to-face meetings with managers and buyers and, in many cases, countless rejections. You're not behind the security of your computer screen anymore, and you'll have to be a salesman in person. But unlike selling in person at a street fair, you'll have to convince someone to purchase not one or two but dozens of your products.

Convincing a retailer to make a wholesale order and sell your products in his store can also be easy. If you build your brand to the point that you've made a name for yourself, you might actually have some retailers contacting *you* begging for the privilege to sell your brand in their stores. So, in a way, selling in stores can be a matter of timing.

Consequently, if your brand is relatively unknown, it's likely that you'll have a hard time getting retailers to commit to wholesale orders. Or if you do manage to seal some retail accounts, your products might collect dust on shelves for months since none of the stores' customers have heard of your brand and would prefer buying something they recognize.

When the time is right for you to start your hunt for potential retail stores, here's what you'll need to do to achieve the best results. But remember, no matter how good your brand is or how much you plan your approach, you will always be faced with some rejection along the way. Just learn to brush it off and keep on moving.

Narrow It Down

Before starting your hunt for possible retail locations, consider specifying the types of stores that would be the best fit for your brand. It's not a good idea to just go for any store that is willing to place an order. First and foremost, all of your potential retail spots should be stores that you would be proud to have your brand available in. Make sure to keep an eye out for online retail shops that sell products from multiple brands as well. Furthermore, each store should be frequented by your target market. It doesn't help to be in a store if your intended customer doesn't even shop there.

The easiest way to narrow down the retailers you should aim to sell to is by referring to the brands you consider somewhat similar to your own in terms of style and intended audience. (Note: If your brand is in no way similar to *any* other brand, you might be doing something wrong!) Find out which stores these similar brands are available in, and compile a list of the ones you feel would suit your brand. Most brands list their retailers on their website, on a page titled "Retailers" or "Stockists," so this should be easy to find. If your brand is similar to another brand carried by a retailer, it's easier to convince the retailer that your products would sell in his store.

For starters, make a list of at least ten stores you can see your brand in. Be sure to list each store's contact information and address. You can even aim for online stores, some of which work on drop shipping terms (**Karmaloop.com** for example). Drop shipping basically means your products are up for sale on the store's website, and as orders come in you fulfil them yourself (rather than the store having your products in stock). Which ever stores you choose to aim for, be sure to do your research.

Creating A Catalog Or Line Sheet

When approaching clothing retailers, you'll need, among a few other things, a line sheet or catalog to show what your brand has to offer. A line sheet is a sheet of paper that shows your line of t-shirts and information for making a wholesale purchase. This can also come in the form of a multi-page catalog. Most clothing brands create a new catalog or line sheet every few months to reflect new collection releases. Here's what to include in your line sheet or catalog.

Images Of Each Product

Most line sheets show computer-generated mock-ups of each product, not photographs, because this makes the design clearer. Show all important views of your t-shirt. For example, if you have graphics on the front and back, show both sides. If there are small details in your graphic, show a close up of the detail. Represent your designs in the best way you can.

Style Names and Numbers

You can use a sequence of numbers, letters, or a combination of both. Make your style numbers easy to remember, for you and for the buyer. Using a formula can make it easy. Some companies use a number from 1-9 to represent things like fabric, color, design and size, and put them in a select order.

Wholesale and Retail Prices

List both the wholesale and suggested retail price of each t-shirt. Remember, the wholesale price is usually half of the suggested retail price. Locating the pricing of each t-shirt should be easy, so design and organize the layout of the sheet straightforwardly and intuitively.

Colors and Fabric Information

List important details about the fabric each t-shirt is made of. Also show the colors each shirt is available in. If a design is available in multiple colorways, show the design in each color if possible.

Delivery Dates and Order Cut-Off Dates

You must also state delivery dates and order cut-off dates. The delivery date is when the retailer can expect his order to be delivered (based on your production time), and the order cut-off date is the last day the retailer can place his order. This info needs to be at the top of your line sheet or in a prominent section in your catalog.

Order Minimums

List your order minimum, which is basically the smallest number of products a retailer can purchase from you. You can list a minimum per t-shirt design as well as a minimum total order. For example, 5 pieces per design, $250 per total order.

Contact Information

This is obviously very important. List this clearly in a prominent place, or you won't be getting any callbacks.

Order Form

Include an order form along with your catalog or line sheet to enable the retailer to place an order on the spot, or as soon as he makes up his mind. Make space to allow the retailer to mark off styles, sizes and quantities, as well as his shipping and contact info. Take a look at other companies' catalogs to see an example of this. Make the order process as easy and painless as possible.

Product Samples

Put together a package of three or more product samples to give potential retailers. Despite your well-designed line sheet or catalog, a retailer might not feel ready to commit to a purchase until he sees a physical sample of your product. This is where the quality of your products is important. Your designs might look good on paper, but if they don't look as good in physical form, you can get turned down. That's why it's necessary to always create high-quality products.

Add your catalog or line sheet, along with some business cards and some additional information about your brand, to this sample package and send it out to your retailers of choice. Giving out all this stuff for free will cost you, but it's a price you should be willing to pay if you really want to get into these stores. Take advantage of any opportunity you have to meet with retailers in person so you can show off your product samples face to face.

Order Payment Terms

When it comes to wholesale transactions, payment isn't as simple as it is for online sales. There are different types of payment terms involved, including *net 30* (retailer pays you 30 days after receiving your products) and *COD* (cash on delivery). It's important to decide in advance which terms you will offer and accept so that you're not pushed to agree to whatever the retailer wants. In some cases, you may have to be flexible depending on how badly you want to be in a specific store, but generally it's good to only agree to terms you can afford to work with.

When starting out, you might be tempted to agree to consignment terms, under which you give your products to retailers to sell in their stores and you only get paid if your products sell. This is a bad idea, a deal you should stay away from. I've heard consignment nightmare stories from far too many brands. There's no guarantee that you'll get paid even if your products do sell. Consignment is usually offered by a retailer when your brand hasn't made a name for itself yet and the retailer isn't confident in investing money in your brand. This is why it's important to properly time your retail efforts.

What you should aim for when sealing retail deals is pre-payment; that way, your payment is guaranteed. COD is also a good deal, under which the retailer must present a check for the total order amount upon delivery. Under any other terms, there's a chance you might be left with no payment after giving away your products. If no retailer is willing to pay for your products in advance, maybe it's not the right time for you to try getting into stores. In that case, work on further developing your brand to the point that it is in high demand, and then give it another go.

Jing Liu On Getting Into Stores

Getting into stores was one thing that I couldn't find any information or advice about at the beginning. If you have ever tried to get your brand into stores, you probably were like me and couldn't even get a meeting with a buyer. How the heck would I get my brand into stores if the buyer wouldn't even see me? I asked other brand owners but did not get any good information. There are two good reasons as to why. One is that others didn't have much success themselves, and the other is that they didn't want to share their secrets.

My brand, **JUZD** (pronounced "juiced"), has been in over 40 boutiques within two years. The good news for you is that you won't need to go through all the hardship and rejection I went through to crack the code. I will share with you right here all the secrets that helped me get into those stores.

I will distill below the most efficient path to getting your line into a boutique. The goal is to focus on the stores you want to get into and pursue those with a lot of your energy rather than targeting many stores with an unfocused energy.

1) Research the stores you want to be in.

The best way is to look at brands similar to yours and see what stores they are in.

2) Identify the buyers and the managers.

The best way is to call and ask who the buyer is and if you can speak to him or her. If you can get an appointment, get their name and try to see when the buyer is usually in. A little courtesy and respect will get you far.

3) Woo the staff.

This is probably the most important step. It is also the easiest. If you are able to convince the staff to jump on your brand, they will give you access to the buyer. In addition, the buyers always ask the staff for their feedback before picking up a brand. For smaller boutiques, the person who makes the decisions is part of the staff.

4) Ask for the buyer.

Now, if the staff is on board, they will pass you to the buyer or tell you how to get in contact with the buyer. They will help you and champion your brand. It's very important to act as if the buyer is expecting you. If you found out the name of the buyer, then you can drop that info. Say "John Smith told to me to come by to see my brand." Most likely, the buyer will see your brand, even if only to find out who they booked and why they missed it on their schedule.

Once you are in front of the buyer:

1) Make sure you have all the material you will need:

      a. Line sheet (mock-ups of all your shirts with ordering details)

      b. Lookbook (Photography of your clothing on models. *Optional.*)

      c. Product samples

2) Start with quick chit chat.

Don't talk about random things, but gather important information by asking questions such as "What's your buying direction?" and "What brands sell well?" This info will help you tie in your brand.

3) Talk about your story.

Make sure you have a story! A brand is more than just ink on clothing. It's a story, and I've made many mistakes in the past and missed out by not expressing the story behind my brand. Buyers love it because they know that the staff will be using your story to sell your products. And ultimately, the customers will be enticed because of your story. It's an element that will push your brand over.

4) Ask for the order.

A high percentage of the time the buyer will place the order then and there. Other times, they might need to consult with their partner or get feedback from a particular staff member. If they do need to show it to someone else, ask them when they would be in, and tell them that you would love to present to them as well.

5) Follow up, follow up, follow up.

You want to keep your line in the heads of the buyer, so make sure to get a date by which you should follow up (usually a few days to a week); oftentimes the shorter the period, the more interested they are. If you follow up and they told you that they haven't decided yet, that's actually a good sign. Make sure to ask when the next follow-up should be and do it! So many people flake out. Some people don't know how close to a "yes" they actually are.

6) A "no" is not set in stone.

Even stores that want to pick up your line will sometimes say no. There are many reasons for this. If you cannot convince them, make sure to ask when their buying period is, or when would be a good time to follow up, and follow up as they describe. Timing is everything. If you have a great product and bad timing, they won't pick up your brand. If you have a good product and the right timing, they *will* pick up your brand. Also, many buyers need to see your brand several times and become more familiar with you before they buy.

That is the step-by-step guide I compiled out of my many successes and failures. I hope it will help you avoid as many of the latter as possible.

Jing Liu is the founder of Juzd
(www.Juzd.com)

14

MANAGING YOUR BUSINESS

After launching your t-shirt brand, you have to be able to run it smoothly so that it becomes successful and stays successful. Managing your business is similar to taking care of a car. You don't just save up the money, buy the car and that's it. After you get a car, you have to maintain it; you have a new set of responsibilities. Running a business also gives you a set of responsibilities that go beyond the start-up phase.

Finding Partners

An essential part of running a successful t-shirt brand is having a good executive team. Although that sounds a bit technical and intimidating, having a good executive team means nothing more than going into business with the right people, people who are motivated and committed to reaching the goals of the business,and have the skills (or are willing to develop the skills) necessary to make the brand successful.

You don't need to go all crazy and try to build a team of CFOs, marketing experts and human resources managers. A team can consist of as few as just two people. When launching **Cashletes**, the team basically consisted of two brothers. Neither of us had any real business experience or managerial skills, though it did help that we were both great graphic designers and illustrators. Even though we lacked business skills and experience, we did have the determination to make our brand succeed, and we made sure to do the necessary research, create plans, and put them into action.

It's better to start off with at least one partner, but no more than three. Having too many partners might cause unnecessary conflicts, and you might end up not really getting anywhere with your brand. By having a moderate number of business partners, you'll be able be to stay motivated since you can encourage each other. There's also the benefit that each partner will have some skills or knowledge that they can contribute to the building of the brand.

You might have one guy who's an outstanding graphic designer and another guy who has experience working with social network marketing for fashion-related companies. Combined with your own skills, that could make for an awesome team. To get started on finding partners for your t-shirt brand, create a list of 5-10 friends, family members or acquaintances that might be interested in partnering with you. Then look at the list you created and evaluate each person you listed, asking yourself the following questions:

1) What can this person offer to the development of the brand?

2) What skills does this person have?

3) Is this person usually positive and optimistic about life?

4) Do I generally get along with this person? Does this person respect my ideas?

5) How are the work habits of this person? Is this person focused when working and gets things done, or is this person a slacker?

6) Would running a t-shirt brand be something that this person would actually enjoy?

7) Do I have a basic sense of trust in this person?

After evaluating the people you listed based on such a set of questions, cross out people who don't pass the evaluation criteria. Consider your chemistry with each person as well, because it also has a great impact on a partnership. For example, you might have listed your cousin as a potential partner because he has worked in a retail clothing store and would possibly like the idea of running a t-shirt brand, but if he always complains about life and seems to put you down a lot, it wouldn't make sense to partner with him. Personal issues such as those can leak into your business and become business issues. On the other hand, you might have a friend who's great at drawing cartoons, always tries to see the positive in situations, and generally encourages your ideas. This friend seems like a much more suitable candidate as a business partner.

But what if you don't know anyone who fits the criteria of a good business partner? Maybe everyone in your family is negative and all your friends are slackers. If this is the case, you should explore some other alternatives to finding people to team up with. Sites such as ***PartnerUp.com*** and ***YoungEntrepreneur.com*** are online communities in which you can network with other people interested in starting their own businesses or getting involved in start-up businesses. People on these sites are usually motivated individuals who can serve as great business partners. If you plan on going this route, try to stick to local people so that you can actually hold meetings.

Starting Off Solo

If you've exhausted all of your potential partner options and can't find anybody who's trustworthy, skillful or willing to start a t-shirt brand with, the remaining option would be to go into business solo. There are actually many successful t-shirt brands out there that were started by one guy who was able to take his brand to the top. It just takes more work, and you'll have to make more sacrifices.

In the beginning, you might find it manageable to start off handling certain aspects of building your brand, such as initialization of the branding, designing products, and setting up your site. And, of course, the benefit of starting solo is that you have 100% ownership of your brand. But you'll soon realize that if you want your brand to really get anywhere, you'll need to bring some other people on board to help you.

Hiring People

After running your business for a while and making some progress, you'll start to feel that you could use some help keeping your business alive. You may be waist-deep in work and realize that it's time to either hire people or risk a breakdown from being overworked. Even if you're not overworked, there's a good chance that there are several people out there who can do one of the many jobs you're doing much better and much faster than you can, allowing you time to get more done.

But before you go out and hire a bunch of people to start working for you, you need to decide which responsibilities you could use help with. Start by making a list of all of your current responsibilities.

Your list of responsibilities may look something like this:
- Package orders
- Ship orders
- Create t-shirt designs
- Prepare designs for printing
- Create blog posts
- Create and send newsletter messages
- Promote/network on Facebook and Twitter
- Customer service/respond to e-mails
- Set up promotional events

As your business starts to grow, it's good to know what responsibilities need to be delegated to someone else to take care of. There are different routes you can take when it comes to hiring people or delegating responsibilities. You can either have employees who work with you on a day-to-day basis, or you can outsource specific tasks to a company that specializes in them.

For example, when it comes to packaging and shipping, you can either hire a full-time employee whose responsibility is to package, ship and process orders, or you can outsource the work to a fulfillment company that stores your inventory at a warehouse and handles order processing and shipping. For your promotional efforts, you can either bring a full-time employee on board who handles social network marketing and newsletter promotion, or have these responsibilities delegated to a marketing firm.

When hiring people or contracting work, you'll also have to decide how you'll pay these people while still keeping your business profitable. You will have to sacrifice a bit of your profits to bring on the extra help that will take your business to the next level, but be careful not to put yourself in a situation where you're making no profit at all, or even worse, losing money. Set a budget that falls in line with the income level of your business. The point of hiring people to work for you is to help you increase sales, whether immediately or in the near future. Keeping this in mind, the sacrifice of paying employees to help improve your business will benefit you in the end.

Working With Freelancers

Freelancers are people who sell their services on an independent basis and aren't committed to a single company. These people can be website coders, graphic designers, writers, photographers, and many other specialists. Using sites such as **Guru.com** or **Elance.com**, you can easily find people from around the world who provide the services that you need to help you get your brand off the ground.

However, be careful not to hire someone on the basis of price alone. There are people who charge a low amount for great services, but when you see someone who charges way below the average for their freelance work, you should question how well they will perform. Cheap rates often equal cheap service unless proven otherwise.

Freelancers who charge low rates and seem to have a great portfolio are either newcomers or people from developing nations. For example, e-commerce shop design and coding will generally cost you over $800, but you might be able to get a site design done by a graphic designer from India for only $400. But when choosing international freelancers, you may have to deal with communication difficulties (since they may not be not native English-speakers) or slight delays in the completing the task (with conflicting time zones). But in the end, the work can turn out to be satisfactory.

It can still be a risk to work with "low ballers," but at the same time, you don't want to work with "rip-off artists" either. People who charge astronomical rates can be just as low-quality as those charging rock-bottom rates. As a general rule, evaluate multiple freelancers. Ask for their rates, check out their previous work, and compare all these aspects to decide who to hire. Since freelancers won't have a stake in your business or have any control of it, it's not important that you actually meet them in person to work with them. You can conduct all communication online or over the phone if necessary.

When assigning work, make sure that you're very clear in explaining exactly what you need done. Being freelancers ourselves, we know what it's like to deal with vague clients. Back when we first started designing websites, we had a difficult client who owned a t-shirt brand. The client had a basic idea of how he wanted his site to look, but he was very vague about the kind of layout, color scheme, and font style he wanted to use. Every time we showed him a site mock-up for approval, he would give a vague suggestion, such as "try making it look a bit different," without elaborating on what "different" meant to him.

As a result, we ended up designing more than ten different site mock-ups, none of which were fully approved or given clear feedback on what needed to be changed. To add to that, he was very disengaged about his own project, even stating that he didn't have time to deal with the project and that since we're the designers, we should know what to do.

In the end, he got frustrated (and so did we) and decided to stop working with us. He even tried filing a PayPal claim to get his deposit back (PayPal took our side) and threatened to badmouth our company. Now, after three years, he's left with the same boring site design he had when he came to us, and from the looks of it, his brand is inactive. All this could have been avoided if he'd just given clear instructions when assigning the project.

The lesson here is to make things easier for yourself and everyone involved. Don't be *that* client. Make the details of your project very clear to the freelancers you're working with, and have realistic expectations of what can be accomplished.

After getting a good feel for a freelancer and their rates, decide if you want to work with them. It's also a good precaution to pay a 50% down payment for a project. Freelancers will usually request a 50/50 payment term anyway. If you have a freelancer do some t-shirt designs for you, consider having him design your website, too. If you like his work and the first project goes smoothly, you should continue to assign new projects to the freelancer and establish a relationship. Although the freelancer won't be an official partner, they will function as an important part of your team and contribute to your brand's success.

Customer Service

An important aspect in managing your brand is customer service. Customer service basically consists of the way the customer is "treated" before and after he purchases and receives a product. You want to be able to provide your customers with a great shopping experience and give them a good impression about your brand to keep them coming back.

Before the Purchase

Often times, people who are interested in your brand will contact you before they make a purchase. Maybe someone has a question about your delivery times or the sizing of your t-shirts. Customers who contact you before making a purchase want to make sure that the product they are going to buy will arrive by the time they expect it and in the condition they expect it to be in.

A good way to handle all of these pre-purchase customer concerns is to make sure to provide detailed answers to these potential questions in an FAQ section on your website. You can refer back to the "Set Up Shop" chapter for ideas on what questions and answers to include in your FAQ. Being able to answer a majority of customer concerns on your FAQ page will make it easier for your customers to get the information they need to feel comfortable making a purchase. It will also reduce the number of e-mails you get from people asking the same questions over and over.

Shipping Orders

After the customer's pre-purchase concerns have been dealt with and he decides to make a purchase, you'll have to be able to answer any concerns the customer may have after his product has been shipped. A common issue that tends to arise is the question of when an order will arrive. Although you may have stated your delivery times, if an order is taking longer than usual to arrive to the customer, he may begin to get a bit restless.

To avoid this from happening in the first place, make sure to get orders in your shipping carrier's hands within 24 hours of the customer ordering. On top of that, make sure you provide customers with package tracking numbers. Every shipping carrier provides these, so you should have no problem getting a tracking number assigned to each order. Every online shop I've ever ordered from has informed me of my tracking number, so I expect one every time. Your customers will expect one, too, so it's important to always provide one.

A good way to ensure that packages are always shipped on a timely basis is to sign up for package pick-up with your shipping carrier of choice. Most shipping carriers offer this as well, but we recommend using **USPS** (if you live in the United States) based on their very affordable rates for shipping t-shirts. You want to make sure that your shipping costs don't eat up your profits, and in our experience, USPS is usually the best choice.

Another option to ensure that packages are shipped as soon as possible is to have an order fulfillment company handle your orders. By using a fulfillment company to ship your orders, you'll be able to ship orders out faster and handle shipping a larger quantity of orders than if you were to do the shipping yourself. Since customers will generally receive their orders a little faster, they will feel more satisfied with their shopping experience and may consider buying from you again in the future.

Shipping Delays and Issues

You might ship orders quickly and supply tracking information with every order, but there are still potential delays that are relatively out of your control. If you have international customers, then you'll definitely encounter a situation in which a customer still hasn't received an order after three weeks or more. Consequently, the customer will become understandably frustrated. You have to be able to assure the customer that the product will arrive soon, or you'll ship out a new one.

Let's say you shipped a t-shirt out to a customer in France, and you're based in the U.S. The normal expected delivery time for USPS First Class International shipping is two to three weeks, but four weeks have gone by and the customer has yet to receive his product. A problem like this isn't your fault, but it becomes your responsibility to deal with it. Most likely, the customer will e-mail you requesting the status of his order.

When that happens, you should respond to the customer informing them about the reason for the delay and asking them to give the package another two weeks to arrive. This isn't what the customer wants to hear, but there's virtually nothing you can do to speed up the shipping process once it's already been shipped. If after *another* 2-3 weeks the customer contacts you about *still* not receiving the product (and you also checked the tracking information to confirm that it has yet to be successfully delivered), it would be a good idea to offer a refund for the cost of the purchase, since the package may be lost at this point.

This would be the right thing to do, since the customer has yet to receive a product that he paid for weeks ago. What we sometimes do in a situation like this is give a refund *and* ship the product out again. We often win back angry customers this way. When a package does end up being lost, you can regain the costs of shipping the lost product by filling a claim with your shipping carrier, giving information about the lost package and requesting a refund.

Returns, Refunds and Exchanges

Okay, so you shipped the t-shirt to the customer, it was received on time, and you now have a happy customer. Or so you thought. Now the customer contacts you about returning the t-shirt. Maybe the customer thought the shirt looked darker in the pictures on your site, or perhaps the shirt just didn't fit the way the customer assumed it would fit. Or maybe there was nothing wrong with the shirt, but the customer decided that he needed the money he used on the shirt for something else.

Whatever the reason may be for the return, you'll have to deal with the issue at hand. A return is something that you probably don't want to happen at all, but it comes with the territory of selling things that have a return policy. You might be thinking, "How about making my t-shirts non-refundable?" Making a product non-refundable is only appropriate for certain types of products.

Specifically digital products, like music downloads or website templates. But when it comes to t-shirts, returns must be allowed under certain conditions.

Remember, your customers don't get the opportunity to try your t-shirts on before buying them, so they're taking a risk by making a purchase in the first place. Offering the option to return a product is common practice in the apparel industry, even if you're selling products offline in a physical store. The standard policy for returns is to allow the customer 7-30 days after receiving the product to return it, as long as all hang tags are still in place and the product hasn't been worn.

Sometimes you may be able to counter-offer a return with an exchange of equal value. This way, you don't really lose any money, since you don't have to refund the customer. In cases in which the customer ordered a shirt that was too tight or there was a printing error in the shirt, the customer would be happy to send the shirt back for an exchange, especially if you offer to cover shipping costs. So it's a win-win situation for both of you.

On the other hand, there are situations in which the customer just wants to make a return and get a refund. If your counter-offer has been declined, don't bother trying to push harder for an exchange. Just accept the return, and refund the customer's money. In the case of a return, it's a good idea to ask why the customer decided to return the shirt. This will give you an idea of what you need to improve in order to lower the frequency of merchandise returns.

Additional Thoughts on Customer Service

When dealing with your customers' questions, especially after an order has been made, you want to balance being fair to the customer and being fair to your business. When your customer is unsatisfied about a purchase or is just really worried about his order delivery status, you'll have to decide what the right thing to do is. You have to decipher between a customer complaint being undoubtedly unreasonable or absolutely appropriate and figure out how to address the issue.

Sometimes a customer will have a legitimate complaint that you can't brush off as being unreasonable. These are the situations where you may have made a mistake somewhere along the line. Once we had a customer complain that a product was defective, with some ink stains on the sleeves. As you can imagine, he wasn't impressed. This was a very rare case, and the first time we ever had a customer bring up this type of issue in our entire brand history. The mistake we made along the line was not paying close attention to quality control.

Since we pride ourselves on selling high-quality products, we felt that the right thing to do was give him a full refund while allowing him to keep the product anyway. To our surprise, the customer enthusiastically responded back to us with his appreciation of us giving him a full refund and expressed his respect for our company. He even said that because of how we handled the situation, he'll consider buying even more products from us in the future and will recommend us to his friends. We knew we did the right thing, but we were pretty floored by his response. We came to the conclusion that if you treat your customers right, they'll treat you right.

However, everything isn't so black-and-white. Sometimes there's a gray area. A customer might complain about a t-shirt with a minor printing issue, not even asking for a refund, but just wants to bring this problem to your attention. In a case like this, something like a 20% special discount on their next purchase would be appropriate. A good way to know how to handle all of these different customer issues is to come up with your policies in advance. If you know ahead of time how to handle each type of possible customer issue, customer service will be far less stressful and you'll be able to run your business more effectively.

Fulfillment Services

Just to briefly clarify things, we're not referring to sites like Cafepress and Spreadshirt—the print-on-demand fulfillment companies. The fulfillment services we're recommending take the packaging and shipping workload off of your shoulders and do the work for you. All you have to do is get your t-shirts printed and sent out to the fulfillment warehouse to package, label and ship your products as orders come in. The advantage of using a fulfillment company to handle your orders is that they will save you a large amount of time and energy, allowing you to focus on more important things, such as marketing.

As a new brand, it's not totally necessary to use a fulfillment company as soon as you start. It's actually best to handle all of the preparation, packaging and shipping on your own for a couple months. This way, you get to "set the tone" for how your packaging will be done and figure out your shipping and return policies. Also, if you haven't received any orders yet, you should definitely wait until you get a constant flow of sales before having your stock handled by a fulfillment company.

We'd recommend using a fulfillment company once you're averaging more than one product sale per day (or 30 product sales a month). At this point, you can begin searching for and contacting different fulfillment services. Thirty sales per month isn't a huge amount, but it's a good idea to properly set up your business at the first signs of growth rather than wait several months or years, at which point it can become difficult to handle on your own.

When deciding on a fulfillment company to work with, the main factors that you should look for are cost per order, storage cost, and the type of industries they work with. There are a few costs associated with the fulfillment of an order. Usually the price structure considers the following:

– Charge per order (flat fee for each order)
– Charge per unit (per shirt in the order)
– Handling/small package handling
– Hang tagging charges
– Poly-bagging charges

The total price range for fulfilling an order, assuming that you're shipping only one t-shirt per order, is $2 to $5, taking all costs into consideration. You should aim towards choosing a fulfillment service that charges $3.50 *max* per order in order to stay profitable. You can't afford to have your profits cut heavily by fulfillment charges. At the same time, adding a couple extra dollars to your expense per product for the convenience and benefit of fulfillment will pay off.

Fulfillment companies also usually charge storage fees, since your stock will be taking up space in their warehouse. If you choose a fulfillment company that doesn't have any minimum stock or order requirements, you may only be required to pay as low as $20 per month for storage.

While searching for different fulfillment companies to work with, you'll see that some specialize in serving certain industries while still being able to handle the needs of other types of businesses. It's definitely a smart idea to choose a fulfillment company that states specialization in e-commerce or apparel businesses. Specializing in both would be optimal.

Most fulfillment companies will offer you a back-end system that you can log into online to see detailed data about your products and orders. Once the fulfillment company has your products in their warehouse and the stock count is registered in their system, there are multiple ways that you can notify the fulfillment company about new customer orders that need to be shipped. Some shopping cart platforms offer automatic methods of doing this, while with others you may have to contact your fulfilment company manually.

One of the main concerns that you might have with a fulfillment company handling your orders is the trust factor. You might be thinking, "Can I trust this company to package my products the way I want them to be packaged? Can I trust them to store my products correctly? Are they going to actually ship my stuff on time? What if they steal some of my products?" We certainly had concerns such as these that made us hesitant to use fulfillment services at first. The good news is that fulfillment companies are generally trustworthy and can handle your needs properly. Of course, they won't always be mistake-free, but neither are you.

Having A Solid Work Environment

If you're like most start-up entrepreneurs, you're most likely running your brand from home. A basement, a garage or even a bedroom has been the first office of many entrepreneurs. Having the privilege to work from home is the dream for many people in the professional work force, so you can consider yourself lucky. Wherever it is that you work, it must be a good place to actually get work done. Having a solid work environment will be one of the most important factors in getting your brand off the ground.

Our Work Environment Story

When we first started our brand, we would work from our bedrooms at home. We would basically sit at our laptops all day and try to get as much work done as we could. When nobody else was in the room, this worked out okay. But then our little cousins would come to visit and our parents would force them to stay in our rooms. Imagine sitting at your computer trying to focus on creating a marketing plan while you have a bunch of eight-year-old kids jumping on your bed and screaming at each other.

Or sometimes our mom would ask us to do chores while we were in the middle of a meeting. After getting fed up with dealing with distractions like these, we decided we needed a quiet area to work in. So we decided to start working in our school's library. This gave us the focus that we needed to get real work done. We were able to hold meetings and decide on tasks that needed to be done to reach our objectives.

Our productivity was much higher after deciding to start working in the library, and this showed in our results. But we had to take it up a notch to make even more progress. At the library, we also had to deal with a new set of distractions and, in once case, even theft. On top of that, the library's hours didn't always work with our schedule, so usually we found ourselves having to work from home some days anyway and deal with the same distractions.

So we decided to save up to get our own office. At the time of getting an office, our business was just doing okay, and anyone could have argued that we didn't *need* an office, especially since we weren't a successful business yet. We saved up just enough money to get the office and some furniture. Once we got our office, we were virtually flat broke!

But soon we started to see a rise in our productivity when working from our office. We were able to get way more work done at the office, so we didn't have to bring our work home and struggle through hours of poor concentration. Our product sales started to rapidly increase, and we were able to ship products to customers much faster than before, since we scheduled for USPS pick-up. We were way more organized and focused, and our business started to become successful as a result. On top of that, having the office made us much more motivated, and we enjoyed the new work space.

Establishing Your Work Environment

Running a t-shirt brand is similar to running any other business; you need to be focused to be able to get things done. If you're constantly faced with distractions and have to work in an uninspiring environment, you can spend all day and night working and end up not accomplishing much.

If you don't have many financial resources, you'll need to get creative in establishing a suitable work environment. In the case that your only option is to work from home, make sure to establish a home office. Clear some space in your bedroom or living room to set up a a mini office. Keep your work environment distraction-free, so if you live with other people, establish work hours and get everyone else on the same page. You may be home, but you'll be in work mode during those hours, and you can't have people blasting the TV volume or having loud conversations around you.

Another good idea for establishing a solid work environment on a budget is to go to your nearest public library and do your work from there. The benefit of getting your work done at the library versus working from home is that you're able to more easily separate your work environment from your non-work environment. By doing this, you'll get yourself into work mode when you go to the library, and you can relax when you're done with your tasks and go home.

If you can afford it, rent office space. Renting an office has been one of the best moves we've made in developing our business. Not only does it give you a better work environment, it also gives off a more professional impression. And if you're tired of storing all those boxes of t-shirts in your bedroom, an office will give you a new storage space. You don't need a huge office, as long as you've got enough room to set up essential furniture such as a desk, chair and drawers. Also consider space for your inventory, or a product display. Besides the basics, make sure to give your space a personal touch so that you enjoy working there.

Check online for local listings of office space for rent in your area. Expect to pay a security deposit of two to three times the monthly rent in addition to the first month's rent payment. While getting an office is an additional expense that will initially cost you money that could have been used for production or marketing, the benefit of improved productivity will make up for it.

Tamera Lawerence's Business Management Process

SingleTease launched in March 2007 with just one line of products—our women's *SingleTee* t-shirt. At the time, we were two business partners working on different coasts: one in D.C. and one in L.A. As graphic designers by trade, we continued to work with our own design clients as we slowly built our personal retail brand, SingleTease.

Working from home provided the flexibility we needed to juggle two companies and deal with the time-zone difference. We each employed interns to help us with social media, building our presence on Twitter and Facebook. As a virtual team, we met weekly via **Skype** video chat, and **Google** became our virtual file cabinet and operations backbone.

Fast forward four years. Today, SingleTease has launched a new robust website, expanded to six product lines, and built a robust blog community. To prepare for this growth, one business partner moved from D.C. to L.A. in August 2010.

Now, with the business operating from one central office, we are able to focus as a team on the immediate and long-term goals of the company. Before the transition, collaboration was limited and forward momentum was a struggle. Our momentum has increased four-fold in the last six months, meeting company goals set years prior.

With a small business, our management model has been to divide and conquer. Our team consists of four individuals, two focusing exclusively on social media marketing. Today, the business partners are focusing their efforts on building business affiliations and opportunities to expand our B2C (Business to Consumer) reach, integrating our strategy with the social media team.

As with any small business, the business partners continue to wear many hats. A typical day at the office is dictated by an extensive Google "priorities list." We started this **Google Docs** document in August 2010. All of our operations are color-coded and prioritized in order of importance. Each person on the team has daily, weekly and monthly goals they are required to meet. We have a 90-minute staff meeting every Wednesday to review our progress individually and as a team. We open the last 30 minutes to share ideas, stuff we read about, new apps, etc.

Our virtual list also has a "Completed" column which gives us a virtual pat on the back versus just deleting a task from our list. Accomplishments and stats for the week are listed on a whiteboard for everyone to see and add to as we meet our goals.

In addition to noting our progress within our Google document, each member is required to track his or her time spent working. Twelve categories are available to assign for time spent. We never tracked our time this extensively before August 2010. We're not keeping track for accountability but to analyze how and where we are spending our time. As a small team, we don't have a minute to waste.

For our small business, Google has really made the greatest impact on our operations. We have 200 docs available to our team, from notes on webinars to research on competitors to statistics on our target audience and orientation for our new interns. In addition to our docs, we live and breath by our **Google Calendar**. Beyond meetings, we schedule and track promotions, events, education, and networking events.

We just added two new calendars: our blog and *Twitter* schedules. Everything is in one place and accessible by every team member from any location. All the information we are tracking provides another level of data we can analyze and compare. We are not operating in the dark.

Staying on top of the latest technology can be a full-time job in itself, but it allows us to maximize collaboration and have the greatest impact on our growth. Plus, it allows us to spend more time on what we love—creating more clever products to help singles meet face-to-face!

**Tamera Lawrence is co-founder of Single Tease
(www.SingleTease.com)**

15

KEEP ON
KEEPIN' ON!

At some point you may be down in the dumps, and you'll start to feel like the best thing for you to do is quit or put your brand on hold. But no matter what your situation, don't do it! Just keep up the hard work until it pays off. Yeah, we know "don't quit" and "stay motivated" are as cliche as it gets when it comes to achieving your goals, but it's really important to stay motivated if you want anything to come of this brand you've created.

When You're Feeling Down

After the excitement of your brand's start-up phase, there comes a time when you begin to lose that spark that had you fired up in the beginning. Maybe you launched an ad campaign for your brand that did horribly, or perhaps a few sour readers left some harsh, gut-wrenching comments on an article written about your brand. Or maybe you started looking at all the other cool brands out there and realize your brand sucks compared to them—and to top it all off, your sales numbers prove it. But the most important thing here is to continually do everything you can to improve every aspect of your brand.

Can't Sell Jack

By now you already know that you shouldn't quit at the first sign of defeat. But how about when you've done everything you can to create a kick-ass brand and you *still* aren't seeing any sales? This happens to new brand owners all the time. They work long and hard only to be faced with poor sales numbers, despite having an awesome brand. So what do you do when customers still aren't buying from you, even after your shop has been up for weeks? You need to perform a check-up on your brand.

Is Anyone Visiting Your Site?

As obvious as it sounds, you actually need online traffic to make sales. Just like a store at the mall depends on foot traffic, your online shop depends on web surfers to make their way to your web store. Make sure you install some type of analytics tracker on your site, such as **Google Analytics**, to view your site's traffic stats at the end of each day to make sure that you're actually getting visits.

Try any additional targeted promotion tactics, especially free ones, to get more exposure and gain momentum. Then step back and take a look at what's working and what isn't, and make the necessary adjustments. Use your analytics tracker to monitor the effects of all your efforts.

High Traffic, Still No Sales

Maybe you are getting a lot of traffic, but it's just not converting into sales. It's important to look at your current traffic sources and decide which sources are targeted and which ones aren't. Getting 1,000 visits a day from FreeGames.com when you're selling fishing t-shirts probably won't get you any sales. On the other hand, getting 50 visits a day on a site like FieldAndSteam.com, an outdoors website about hunting and fishing, will most likely get you far better results, with visits turning into sales.

Also, analyze how you're currently ranked on search engines such as Google for the keywords that you're targeting. As a rule of thumb, if you're aiming for the search term "Wacky t-shirts" and your site doesn't show up on the first page of search results, no one is really going to your site by searching for that term. You need to reconfigure your SEO strategy, or consider hiring a professional if all else fails.

High *Targeted* Traffic, *Still* No Sales

In some cases, you'll be visible on targeted sites, rank number-one for your keywords in the search engines, and feel that you are getting a decent amount of traffic, but for some reason the sales just aren't adding up. This is probably a bigger motivation drainer than not getting visitors at all, because when you're not getting visitors at least you know why you're not making any sales. This phenomenon usually happens for two reasons:

A) People are just becoming aware of your brand and need some more convincing before deciding to buy from you.

B) Visitors do want to buy from you and have the money right now to do it, but their having a hard time due to some technical difficulties or concerns about purchasing your products online.

Reason 'A' just requires some patience. The best thing you can do is stay consistent with your current marketing strategy for a few more weeks. Within time, you'll start to turn visitors into customers, if they are indeed target visitors.

Reason 'B,' however, is a technical issue that is completely within your control to fix. A great tactic to check if visitors are having a hard time buying from you is to run a "shopper simulation." Start from your homepage and navigate your site like a potential customer. Go through the process of clicking products, adding them to the cart, and checking out. While doing this, make note of any issues you come across.

Some common issues are being unable to checkout or having a hard time finding the actual shop page. Continually check for issues like these and make modifications to your site functionality accordingly. If you created your site yourself, it may be hard for you to tell if it's difficult to navigate, since in your eyes it's perfect. In this case, you should ask a friend to navigate your site and make a test purchase. Then ask for feedback on the entire purchasing experience.

Keep Your Eyes On The Prize

You might discover that your sales have stagnated and you don't see any growth on the horizon. Or maybe you *are* seeing growth in your business, but you start to lack the motivation to continue working on your brand for some outside reasons. When this happens, remind yourself why you started your brand in the first place. What was the vision you had when entering the t-shirt business? Did you picture your favorite rock band sporting your gear? Did you imagine having an out-of-this-world display at that big trade show you've always wanted to exhibit at? Did you dream about seeing products you designed in stores all over the world? Reminding yourself of your original motivations can help get you back in good spirits.

You should also think about the impact your business can have on your quality of life. Picture yourself driving your dream car to your class reunion, or being able to travel across the world. Imagine being able to party with celebrities, donate thousands of dollars to the charities you support, or simply have financial freedom and more time to spend with your friends and family.

The thing is, to make sure your business becomes successful, you need to keep on visualizing these dreams that you had when starting out so that you have the motivation to keep your business moving. Better yet, just like you should write down your business goals, create a list of your life goals—goals that will be attainable as a result of reaching your business goals. Whenever you feel demotivated, take a look at your list and picture reaching those goals so that you spark that fire again.

Keeping your eye on the prize won't magically solve your business problems and accomplish your goals, but it will give you the extra strength to allow you to create solutions and reach the goals you set.

Reward Yourself Often

A very helpful way to keep yourself on track and motivated on a day-to-day basis is to reward yourself when you do a good job. Just like a boss in a corporation would give employees bonuses for reaching certain sales quotas, you, being the boss of yourself, need to give yourself a bonus for reaching sales quotas. A standard thing that we always do after we reach our revenue goal for the month, or break our own monthly revenue record, is treat ourselves to dinner. On top of that, we write bonus checks to ourselves for a really small percentage of the revenue for the month.

Of course, accomplishing a certain goal is a reward in its own right, but by treating yourself to something like a dinner or a bonus check, you condition yourself to continue reaching your goals, since you'll be rewarded for doing so. Even if your brand is currently struggling in sales but you managed to accomplish something great, you should reward yourself. Something as small as treating yourself to some ice cream can be an reward.

As you may have noticed, these rewards aren't exactly things that you couldn't give yourself without reaching the goal. A caramel banana split or a meal at Hard Rock Cafe isn't exactly extravagant. But disciplining yourself to be rewarded only upon achieving something, even if it's just a tiny accomplishment, encourages you to keep on accomplishing things regularly so you move towards your goals quicker. Basically, reward yourself even before achieving the ultimate goal.

Regan Smith Clarke on Motivation

I got into the t-shirt business because I wanted to share my own personal vision with the world and meet lots of cool people along the way. I don't have the cliché "I just got tired of not seeing any quality designs" answer for you. The truth is, there is a ton of cool stuff around, but there's always room for new concepts and interpretations.

Some advice I like to offer people who are just starting out is to have a strategy for how you plan to sell your products. Uploading some t-shirt mock-ups online and blasting away on Twitter isn't going to cut it. A well thought-out strategy is often multifaceted, so take your time and figure out what works best for your t-shirt brand.

Now that you've got a slick new strategy in place and out of the way, you should have no problem staying focused. Your next move is to get organized. **Regan Smith Clarke** relies heavily on **Google Docs** to keep track of our marketing initiatives, offline events and general items that require action. I've found that this is an incredible way to stay on track. It also helps that there is always something to do—there isn't much time to dick off!

Part of staying motivated is always setting clearly measurable goals. You don't want to be a ship floating without a destination! For my brand and most other t-shirt brands, the build-up to our releases is the culmination of months and months of hard work. As gratifying as it is for the general public to see what we've been working on, it's also motivating to get moving on new stuff.

Another part of staying motivated is not letting the highs and lows get you bent out of shape. Understand that no matter what level your t-shirt brand is at, there will always be peaks and valleys. A lot of younger t-shirt brands have trouble understanding this concept. Don't let those transition periods between releases or events get you down; understand that they are just part of the process.

When things don't go the way you expected them to, you need to figure out what went wrong. Sometimes, it's hard to view things objectively. A good way to solve this problem is to solicit advice from the right people (not your girlfriend/boyfriend, best friend, grandmother, etc.).

If you have a mentor or access to someone who's already established in the business, ask if they can offer you an outside perspective. Remember to thank these people and show your appreciation in the form of buying some of their merchandise. You can also elicit unbiased and anonymous information for free with the help of websites such as ***SurveyMonkey.com*** and ***Formspring.com***, offering a coupon code as an incentive.

Don't jump ship if things don't turn out the way you had hoped. Review your game plan and figure out if you need to tweak it or stay the course. It's pretty easy to glaze over everything with an excuse, but in order to improve, you need to evaluate both your successes and your failures.

Regan is the founder of Regan Smith Clarke
(www.ReganSmithClarke.com)

16

WHAT'S NEXT?

By now, you should have a thorough understanding of what it takes to launch a kick-ass t-shirt brand. From creating a solid brand and producing your products to setting up your shop online and managing your business, we've covered all of the main aspects of building a t-shirt business from the ground up. But there's much more beyond all that.

Beyond T-Shirts

While t-shirts are great products that are easy to get produced and are pretty affordable to the end customer, you're going to need to move beyond t-shirts to further establish yourself as successful brand. A lot of the successful indie clothing brands that you see out there today started with a collection of a few t-shirts, and as the years went by, began adding new products to the mix in order to expand.

The easiest products to start creating after t-shirts are sweatshirts and hoodies. Usually, your screenprinter should already be able to print on these garments, and they can cost anywhere from $2 to $10 more per unit than t-shirts. If it's summer time, it would obviously be harder to sell sweatshirts and hoodies, but adding these products to your fall, winter, and early spring lineups should help boost your product sales and improve your brand perception.

If you don't quite have the funds for sweatshirts and hoodies, you can try the strategy used by a lot of other upstart brands: sell sticker packs and buttons. The good thing about selling these products is that you can get large quantities created at a pretty low cost and use them as an easy up-sell product in your shop. Customers wouldn't mind paying an extra $2 for some stickers if they were already going to buy a t-shirt for $20. However, these products won't significantly improve your sales. There will be more variety in your shop by having these products available, but you're going to eventually need to move beyond them.

You should also consider expanding to offer additional articles of clothing in your brand collection such as jackets, hats, or button down shirts. The items you choose to sell should be based on your brand image. If you're a skate brand, for example, you can add skateboards to your product variety. Keeping that in mind, some items will not be suitable for your brand, although other big brands out there may be selling them. For example, while a brand like **American Eagle** sells sandals, our brand is never going to sell them because the product is incongruent with our branding.

A good way to decide what other products would be suitable for your brand is to look at the way your target customer dresses and take note of the kinds of clothes and accessories he or she is likely to wear. Again, if you and your friends are good reflections of your target customer, it can be easy to decide on future product types based on your own style.

Finding Manufacturers

As mentioned earlier, **Alibaba.com** is great site to find manufacturers for your products. The site serves as a worldwide online marketplace for finding manufacturers for any kind of product you can imagine. If it can't be made by a manufacturer on Alibaba, then it can't be made at all. You can find manufacturers from all over the world who can produce the products you want.

A very important precaution before paying a manufacturer to produce a run of hundreds of your new product is to order a sample. Find at least three different manufacturers who can produce the product you want, and order one sample from each of them. This way, if one or two manufacturers don't create a high-quality product sample, you'll have backup options. The last thing you want to do is place an order for 100 jackets, and when they arrive the stitching looks like it was done by an amateur, the color is off, and the fit is extremely loose.

We've been unfortunate on multiple occasions dealing with manufacturers. We once ordered a sample of a snapback hat which turned out to look completely different from the photos displayed on the manufacturer's website. Instead of getting a nicely structured hat with a sturdy brim, we received a soggy, flimsy, dusty-looking hat that you might find for sale on Canal Street in New York City for $3.

We were unsatisfied with this hat sample. The quality was laughable. When we contacted the manufacturer claiming we must have been sent the wrong hat, they insisted that they *did* send the right hat and that the photo on their website *did* represent the hat we ordered. It was as if they were looking at a different photo than we were. Either that, or they were legally blind. As you can imagine, we didn't place an order with them. What we learned here was to always request photos of your sample before it is sent out to you, to save you time and disappointment.

There was another situation that was even worse. We ordered a varsity jacket sample from three different manufacturers. One manufacturer sent us a jacket sample that was close to what we wanted, but the leather on the sleeves wasn't the quality we wanted. The next manufacturer sent us a jacket sample that was closer to what we wanted, but with some very minor issues. The last manufacturer sent us nothing! To this day, after several months, this manufacturer has yet to send us a jacket sample that we paid for.

When requesting a sample, don't just ask the manufacturer for a sample of a previous job. Request a sample of a custom-made product with your design on it. Just like working with a screenprinter, you'll have to provide the manufacturer with mock-ups of your product along with detailed information on the sizing and fabric to use. If you're not sure what fabric or material you'll need for a specific product, check the label of a product you want yours to be similar to.

You will need to pay two to five times more money per unit to get a sample produced than you would in an order of 25 or 100 units. If the cost per unit for a jacket is $50, the sample jacket may cost you around $100. So if you're getting three jacket samples, it could cost you about $300 total. That might seem expensive for three jacket samples, but it's better than paying $3,000 for several jackets that end up being very low quality.

Even though there are risks associated with ordering a product sample from a manufacturer, these risks are relatively small. The worst that can happen is losing $100 or so on some lousy (or missing) product samples. However, the payoff that you get when things *do* go right can be amazing. The products that we have had manufactured from scratch for our brand, such as our hats and jackets, make up a majority of our sales now. If it wasn't for taking those risks working with our manufacturers, we wouldn't have been able to enjoy the rewards of selling these products.

Collaborations

Once you've established yourself as a serious brand in the industry, you'll meet other serious brand owners who will actually consider collaborating with you. A collaboration basically consists of your brand and another brand working together on one or more t-shirt designs, usually released in limited editions.

Collaborations happen often in the indie clothing industry, especially amongst two or more brands who could greatly benefit each other. In some ways, a collaboration is sort of like a cosign or a seal of approval. When you collaborate with another brand, that brand is communicating to its fans that they should also check out your brand. You'll then be exposed to a whole new set of potential costumers who might have never discovered your brand had it not been for the collaboration.

Produce Good Stuff

The best way to start collaborating with other brands is by continually producing awesome products until you earn the respect of other legit brands. Fellow brand owners know what it takes to make it in the industry, and if they like the work you're doing and notice that you're doing big things with your brand, you'll earn that respect. If your brand hasn't made a name for itself yet, don't bother pitching for a collaboration yet.

Friends With Benefits

People also like to help out their friends, so you can't expect brand owners who don't know you personally to agree on a collaboration that would most likely only benefit you. Attending industry networking events is a good way to meet other brand owners and build friendly relationships. Almost every discussion I've ever had at a networking type of event has involved some sort of suggestion of collaborating. The more you put yourself in those discussions, the more likely you'll end up talking to your favorite brand owner about a possible collaboration that could benefit the both of you.

You might even be able to score a collaboration with a brand outside of the t-shirt industry or on a product that isn't a t-shirt. The basic idea here is to constantly improve your brand, meet other brand owners, get together and make magic. A collaborative release is usually a big success for both parties, so save room in your future planning for one.

Opening Up A Boutique

After you've established yourself as a consistent brand and have accumulated an increasingly large fan base, the next logical step is to take your business to the next level by opening up a brick-and-mortar store (in other words, an offline retail location). The process of securing a location and setting up shop can be just as complicated as the initial launch of your brand.

Budget

Opening up a boutique requires way more money than launching a t-shirt brand and operating online. All the costs involved will vary based on the size and location of your boutique, the exterior and interior design fixtures, and the amount of stock you will keep. (Warning: Do not attempt open up a shop with a small budget. Expect to pay anywhere from $10,000 to $100,000 for a boutique that has the potential to kick ass.)

Location

One of the most critical decisions you'll make when opening up a store is the location of your new sales channel. Many a business has failed because of a poor location choice. When choosing a location, make sure the area is infested with your target market. This is the most important factor. If the people to whom you cater all your marketing and sales efforts aren't even around to walk by your shop, you won't get many customers.

A good way to know if you have a potential customer base in any given area is to see if there are any other shops in the area selling t-shirts or other products similar to yours. If there aren't any, take that as a warning sign that it might not be a good idea to set up shop there. Lack of similar shops in an area could mean your target market doesn't live there, or other similar shops *have* opened in the past, only to fail.

Also be sure to consider the financial demographics of the area. Opening a shop selling t-shirts for $30 each wouldn't fare well in a lower-class neighborhood. Most importantly, pick a location that fits your market, with a lease amount that fits your budget.

Products and Display

Having a physical boutique heightens the importance of stock management. Although managing your stock is important overall, it's even more imperative in a retail store setting. Not only should you try to have every product you offer in stock, you should also try to have every size of every product in stock. The more likely a customer is to find his or her size, the more likely that customer will make a purchase.

When it comes to your store display setup, your shop design should match your branding, inside and out. The name of your brand should be clearly displayed on the outside of the store. On the inside, display your products in an environment that reflects what your brand is all about. It would be awesome to see a jungle-themed brand have its t-shirts hanging from trees in the middle of the store, or an army-themed brand with folded shirts on camouflage-painted shelves with a tank in the corner of the store—anything that looks good and gives people a good impression of your brand.

You don't need anything extravagant either. You can opt for basic storage units and hang framed t-shirt designs all over the walls. Some furniture is always a nice touch, too (and is especially appreciated by those who are waiting while their friends shop). Overall, you should aim for an inviting display that entices people to walk into your shop and potentially make a purchase.

Events, Promotions and Exclusives

To prevent your retail shop from going out of business, keep things exciting by frequently hosting events, running sales and other promotions, and offering in-store exclusives. This kind of marketing helps you attract new customers and keep old ones. Throw a 4th of July barbecue right in your store or a summer block party right out front. Have a 50%-off sale at the start of each season or give out coupons for future purchases. Create limited-edition products that are available only in the store (not online or through any of your other sales channels). Once you've got your own store, there is a plethora of new marketing tactics you can implement.

Building Your Empire

After learning about the trials and tribulations of owning a t-shirt brand, you're probably excited to start your own journey building a t-shirt empire. We encourage you to approach your business endeavour with a sense of informed optimism. Be optimistic about all that you'll achieve with your brand, but also stay informed about what it takes to get there and the challenges and setbacks you'll come across.

Remember, launching and running a t-shirt brand isn't a cakewalk. But if you stay persistent, keep a positive attitude and learn from your mistakes, you'll be able to eventually have your cake and eat it too. You'll be able to pursue your passion and make a living doing so. With the knowledge you've gained from reading this book, you are well on your way to success as a t-shirt brand owner. So get out there and start kicking some ass!

APPENDIX
RESOURCES

Producing Your Products

Product Design

Adobe Photoshop
(www.photoshop.com/)

Adobe Illustrator
(www.adobe.com/Illustrator/)

Pixlr
(www.pixlr.com/)

Screen Printers

Threadbird
(www.threadbird.com/)

Antilogy Design
(www.antilogydesign.com/)

Jak Prints
(www.jakprints.com/)

Clothing Manufacturer Directory

Alibaba
(www.alibaba.com/)

Website Creation Essentials

E-Commerce Solutions

Big Cartel
(www.bigcartel.com/)

Core Commerce
(www.corecommerce.com/)

Big Commerce
(www.bigcommerce.com/)

Shopify
(www.shopify.com/)

Site Designers and Templates

Theme Fiend (Big Cartel themes)
(www.themefiend.com/)

Template Monster
(www.templatemonster.com/)

BrandxHype
(www.brandxhype.com/)

The Neon Hive
(www.theneonhive.com/)

Double Dragon Studios
(www.doubledragonstudios.com/)

The Black Axe
(www.theblackaxe.com/)

Domain Name Registration Sites

Godaddy
(www.godaddy.com/)

Bluehost
(www.bluehost.com/)

1 and 1
(www.1and1.com/)

Website Hosting and Blog Creation

Wordpress Hosting
(www.wordpress.org/)

(via Godaddy services)
(www.godaddy.com/hosting/wordpress-hosting.aspx?ci=15005/)

Tumblr
(www.tumblr.com/)

Newsletter/Mailing List Solutions

Mailchimp
(www.mailchimp.com/)

Constant Contact
(www.constantcontact.com/)

Information and Advice Sites

T-Shirt Community Sites

T-Shirt Forums
(www.t-shirtforums.com/)

Mintees
(www.mintees.com/)

Band Job
(www.bandjob.com/)

Business Community Sites

Young Entrepreneur
(www.youngentrepreneur.com/)

Partern Up
(www.partnerup.com/)

Blogs

T-Shirt Magazine
(www.t-shirtmagazine.com/)

How to Start a Clothing Company
(www.howtostartaclothingcompany.com/)

Legal Resources

Legal Zoom
(www.legalzoom.com/)

Law on the Web (Business Law section)
(www.lawontheweb.co.uk/Business_Law)

Financial

Accounting Software

Outright
(www.outright.com/)

Xero
(www.xero.com/)

Quickbooks
(quickbooks.intuit.com/)

Merchant Solutions

Paypal
(www.paypal.com/)

Amazon Payments
(payments.amazon.com/)

Miscellaneous

Photography and Models

Model Mayhem
(modelmayhem.com/)

Young Photographers United
(ypu.org/)

Tradeshows and Events

Renegade Craft Fair
(www.renegadecraft.com/)

Agenda Tradeshow
(www.agendashow.com/)

Magic Tradeshow
(www.magiconline.com/)

Comic-Con
(www.comic-con.org/)

Management Tools

Google Docs
(www.docs.google.com/)

Wufoo
(www.wufoo.com/)

Dropbox
(www.dropbox.com/)

BRANDING WORK-SHEET

This questionnaire work-sheet will help you develop your brand personality and image. Fill out the answers here or in a "branding notebook". A solid brand is the difference between a successful company and one prone to failure.

1. What products do you offer? Define the qualities of these products.

2. What is the reoccurring theme behind your brand? What kind of messages are you trying to convey through your products?

3. What style of clothing are your products? What kind of stores could you picture your brand in?

4. What colors are prominent in your logo, website, and products?

5. What is the mission of your brand?

BRANDING WORK-SHEET

6. Who is your target market? Describe the kind of people your products attract.

7. What do you want others to know and say about your products or services?

8. Review the answers to the questions above and create a profile of your brand. Describe the personality or character with words just as if you were writing a biography or personal ad.

9. Based on your brand profile, how would you like your target audience to react to your brand?

10. Where can you find potential customers? How will you advertise your brand to them?

BRANDING WORK-SHEET

11. Who are your biggest competitors? What can you do better than them?

12. What does your web site say about your brand? Does it reflect professionalism and clarity while giving a good impression of your brand image?

13. What does your answering system and call return policy say about your brand? Does it say we are here to help, eager for you business and will do what it takes?

14. What's the ONE word you would use that best describes your brand or your products?

T-SHIRT DESIGN TEMPLATE

FRONT

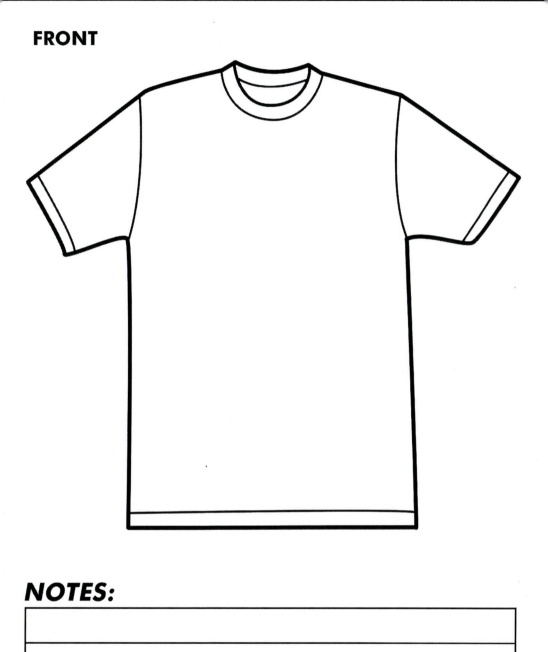

NOTES:

T-SHIRT DESIGN TEMPLATE

BACK

NOTES:

SAMPLE LINE SHEET / CATALOG PAGE

NAME; EMAIL@EMAIL.COM; 555-555-5555
DELIVERY DATE: 10-20 Business Days
ORDER CUT-OFF DATE: Month, Date, 2011

ORDER TERMS: Pre-payment; COD
ORDER MINIMUM: 1 Dozen Per Style

Your Brand

All t-shirts are 6 oz, 100% cotton jersey with front screen printed graphic.
Double needle bottom hem and sleeves. Shoulder-to-shoulder tape.
Preshrunk to minimize shinkage.

PRODUCT 1
SIZES SMALL-2X
$15 WHOLESALE
$30 SUGGESTED RETAIL

PRODUCT 2
SIZES SMALL-2X
$15 WHOLESALE
$30 SUGGESTED RETAIL

PRODUCT 3
SIZES SMALL-2X
$15 WHOLESALE
$30 SUGGESTED RETAIL

PRODUCT 4
SIZES SMALL-2X
$15 WHOLESALE
$30 SUGGESTED RETAIL

SAMPLE ORDER FORM

Your Brand

50 ADDRESS ST
CITY, STATE ZIP
EMAIL@EMAIL.COM
555-555-5555

COMPANY INFO			
COMPANY NAME			
BUYER / OWNER			
ADDRESS			
CITY	STATE		ZIP
PHONE		EMAIL	
DATE	TERMS	50/50 ☐	COD ☐

PRODUCT	PRICE	QUANTITY					TOTAL PRICE
T-SHIRTS		S	M	L	XL	2X	
JACKETS		S	M	L	XL	2X	

PRODUCT	PRICE	$7^{1/8}$	$7^{1/4}$	$7^{3/8}$	$7^{1/2}$	$7^{5/8}$	$7^{3/4}$	$7^{7/8}$	8	TOTAL PRICE
FITTED CAPS										

SIGNATURE:_____

ORDER TOTAL ☐

MINIMUM ORDER IS ONE DOZEN PIECES PER PRODUCT

MAKE CHECKS PAYABLE TO "YOURBRAND" OR MAKE CREDIT CARD PAYMENT ONLINE. PURCHASE IS NON-REFUNDABLE UNLESS GOODS ARE DAMAGED UPON DELIVERY. ORDER CANNOT BE CANCELLED ONCE PROCESSED.

SAMPLE TRADE SHOW APPLICATION

Please include the following with your completed Agreement:

1. The Show Directory/Website Information section
2. The Merchandise Information Form
3. Your company's product line sheet along with a catalog, press kit, brochure and/or photos
4. Make payment online at www.advanstar.com/payonline or make check payable to MAGIC/Advanstar. *(International exhibitors see wire transfer instructions).*

Mailing Address Information:

Please type or print clearly. Do not use Post Office Box Number.

Exhibiting Company Name_____

Address 1_____

Address 2_____

City_____

State_____ Zip_____

Province_____ Country_____

Phone_____

Fax_____

Company Website_____

Key Personnel:

Management Contact / Decision Maker

Name_____

Title (CEO / Pres. / V.P., etc)_____

Phone_____

E-mail_____

Show Contact / Trade Show Coordinator

Name_____

Title (CEO / Pres. / V.P., etc)_____

Phone_____

E-mail_____

PR/Marketing Contact

Name_____

Title (CEO / Pres. / V.P., etc)_____

Phone_____

E-mail_____

Product Development / Sourcing Contact

Name_____

Title (CEO / Pres. / V.P., etc)_____

Phone_____

E-mail_____

Company Information:

Annual Sales Volume for 2007:
○ $0 - $499,000 ○ $500,000 - $999,999 ○ $1 million - $9.9 million
○ $10 million - $50 million ○ $50 million and above

Years in Business: ○ Less than 2 years ○ 2 - 5 years ○ Over 5 years

Does Your Company Export? ○ Yes ○ No

Booth Space Requests:

Requests for booth space will be allotted as available. MAGIC will attempt to honor Exhibiting Company's preferences described in this Agreement, but all decisions regarding exhibitor space, location, neighbors, and configuration are in the sole discretion of MAGIC.

Please sign and date this Agreement (including items noted above) and send to MAGIC to secure your space or package. **Booth deposit MUST accompany Agreement. The remaining 50% must be received no less than 60 days prior to the event.**

EXHIBITING COMPANY SIGNATURE X_____ Date_____
(Authorized by Exhibiting Company)

By signing this Agreement the Exhibiting Company agrees to the MAGIC Show Agreement Terms and Conditions found on the reverse side of this Agreement. Any change in the Exhibiting Company's mailing address, show directory information, brand names or product listings must be requested in writing. YES, by signing above the Exhibiting Company hereby affirmatively consents and agrees to receive (i) facsimile advertisements sent by or on behalf of MAGIC/Advanstar Communications to the facsimile number provided above; (ii) telephone solicitations initiated by or on behalf of MAGIC/Advanstar Communications and directed to the telephone number provided above; and (iii) commercial electronic mail messages sent by or on behalf of MAGIC/Advanstar Communications, its affiliates, lines of business and divisions.

Mail to: MAGIC/Advanstar Communications
Attn: Cash Control Dept.
P.O. Box 6150
Duluth, Minnesota 55806-6150

All inquiries please call (818) 593-5000.

Participation Fee & Deposit Per Booth Package:

Please select **ONE OPTION ONLY** per agreement.

OPTION 1

☐ **Exhibit Space (Only) – min 400 sq ft**

Hardwalls and display fixtures are <u>not included</u> in this option but are required for participation. Exhibit space is for floor space only.

Must be approved by show management. Please send visual of booth for approval. Must comply with attached rules and regulations.

Space Cost Only (including 2,000 watts electrical) $15,980

Deposit Required per Space.................................**$8,000**

Total Number of 400 sq ft Spaces Requested_____

OPTION 2

☐ **Studio (Options)**

Each Studio option includes; garment racks, shelving; one (1) table, three (3) chairs, one (1) booth sign, one (1) wastebasket, one (1) area rug, 500 watts electrical and all set up fees included. Drayage is included for PRODUCT ONLY up to 300 lbs.

Please select form the following standard booth options:

☐ **10' x 10'** **$6,500**
☐ **10' x 20'** **$13,000**
☐ **10' x 30'** **$19,500**

50% deposit is due with contract.

OPTIONS:

Please select from below for a total of **6 fixtures per 10 x 10.**

_____**Shelving** — 9.5" x 39"

_____**Hanging Bar** — 39" long, extends 12" from the wall

Your customer service representative will be in touch after receiving the contract, for exact placement of each fixture, and to answer any questions.

OPTION 3

☐ **Showroom**

Each Showroom option includes; two custom graphic panels, four (4) tables, twelve (12) chairs, two (2) booth signs, four (4) wastebaskets, four (4) area rug, 2,000 watts electrical and all set up fees included. Drayage is included for PRODUCT ONLY up to 1200 lbs.

☒ **20' x 20'** **$24,000**
Deposit Required for Showroom **$12,000**

Comments: (i.e. preferred location, neighbors, configuration)

_____
_____
_____
_____

Exhibitor acknowledges and agrees that it will be solely responsible for (a) all exhibition booth costs and expenses not described above, including, without limitation, all costs and expenses for drayage, additional furniture, additional electrical, cleaning and booth decorations not included in the Booth Package and (b) any other exhibition booth packages or services selected by Exhibitor.